Louise [redacted]

FOLENS IDEAS BANK ENVIRONMENTAL ISSUES

Sue Dale Tunnicliffe

Contents

Folens Publishers

How to use this book

Ideas Bank books provide you with ready to use, practical photocopiable activity sheets for your children **plus** a wealth of ideas for extension and development.

TEACHER IDEAS PAGE | **PHOTOCOPIABLE ACTIVITY SHEET**

Clear focus to the activity.

Background information and other help given.

Suggestions for developing work on the photocopiable sheets.

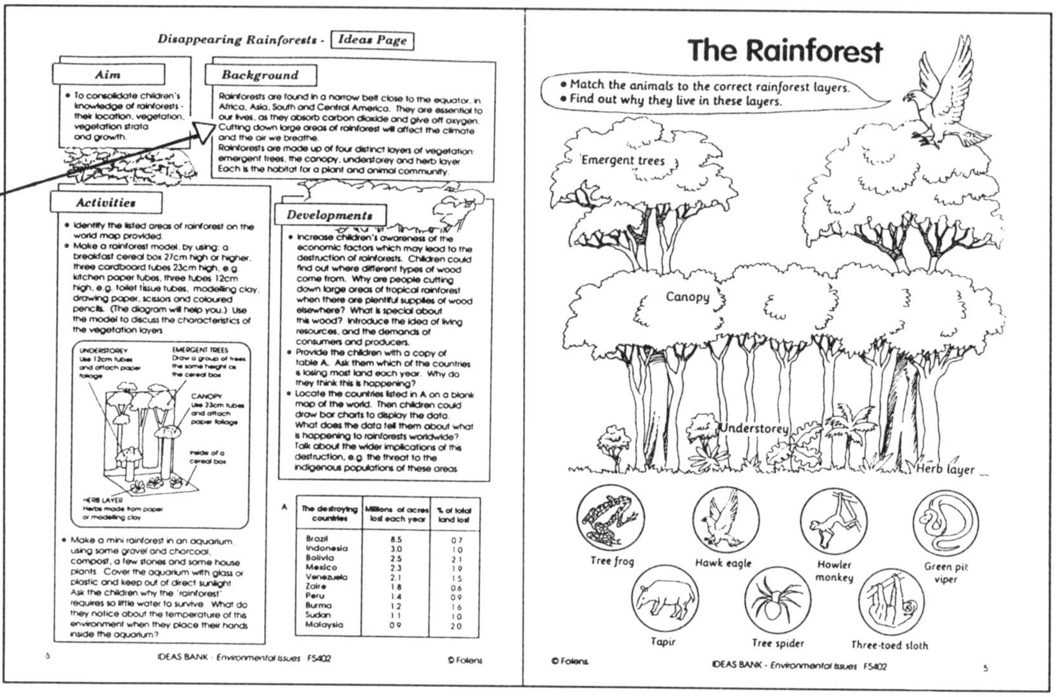

Disappearing Rainforests - *Ideas Page*

Aim

- To consolidate children's knowledge of rainforests - their location, vegetation, vegetation strata and growth.

Background

Rainforests are found in a narrow belt close to the equator, in Africa, Asia, South and Central America. They are essential to our lives, as they absorb carbon dioxide and give off oxygen. Cutting down large areas of rainforest will affect the climate and the air we breathe.
Rainforests are made up of four distinct layers of vegetation: emergent trees, the canopy, understorey and herb layer. Each is the habitat for a plant and animal community.

Activities

- Identify the listed areas of rainforest on the world map provided.
- Make a rainforest model, by using: a breakfast cereal box 27cm high or higher, three cardboard tubes 23cm high, e.g. kitchen paper tubes, three tubes 12cm high, e.g. toilet tissue tubes, modelling clay, drawing paper, scissors and coloured pencils. (The diagram will help you.) Use the model to discuss the characteristics of the vegetation layers.

- Make a mini rainforest in an aquarium, using some gravel and charcoal, compost, a few stones and some house plants. Cover the aquarium with glass or plastic and keep out of direct sunlight. Ask the children why the 'rainforest' requires so little water to survive. What do they notice about the temperature of this environment when they place their hands inside the aquarium?

Developments

- Increase children's awareness of the economic factors which may lead to the destruction of rainforests. Children could find out where different types of wood come from. Why are people cutting down large areas of tropical rainforest when there are plentiful supplies of wood elsewhere? What is special about this wood? Introduce the idea of living resources, and the demands of consumers and producers.
- Provide the children with a copy of table A. Ask them which of the countries is losing most land each year. Why do they think this is happening?
- Locate the countries listed in A on a blank map of the world. Then children could draw bar charts to display the data. What does the data tell them about what is happening to rainforests worldwide? Talk about the wider implications of this destruction, e.g. the threat to the indigenous populations of these areas.

A

The destroying countries	Millions of acres lost each year	% of total land lost
Brazil	8.5	0.7
Indonesia	3.0	1.0
Bolivia	2.5	2.1
Mexico	2.3	1.9
Venezuela	2.1	1.5
Zaire	1.8	0.6
Peru	1.4	0.9
Burma	1.2	1.6
Sudan	1.1	1.0
Malaysia	0.9	2.0

6 IDEAS BANK - *Environmental Issues* F5402 © Folens

The Rainforest

- Match the animals to the correct rainforest layers.
- Find out why they live in these layers.

© Folens IDEAS BANK - *Environmental Issues* F5402 5

Extension activities suggested to take the work one step further.

Independent activities for children to work with.

Time saving, relevant and practical, **Ideas Bank** books ensure that you will always have work readily available.

Acknowledgements

Editor: Angela Simms. Cover by: In Touch Creative Services Ltd. Illustrations by: Tony Dover, Chris Roper and Peter Broadbent.
Cover photo by: The Image Bank. Printed by: Craft Print in Singapore.

First published 1994 by Folens Limited, Albert House, Apex Business Centre, Boscombe Road, Dunstable, LU5 4RL, England.

ISBN 185276540 - 2

Introduction

Concern for the global environment has become one of the most important and controversial issues of the late twentieth century. As the effects of, for example, the destruction of rainforests and the damage to the ozone layer are more widely documented and publicised, a worldwide debate is taking place regarding what measures can be taken to save the planet.

Humans are to blame for many of the factors which are threatening habitats and the species which live in them. We have made such dramatic changes to environments that many living things are unable to adapt. For example, the dumping of chemicals in rivers has killed many freshwater plants and animals. Some living things are now extinct; others are endangered.

Hunting has caused the destruction of species throughout history. In the seventeenth and nineteenth centuries respectively, the dodo and the great auk were hunted to the point of extinction by sailors. Now, although it could be argued that rhinceroses and elephants are nearing the end of their evolutionary span, their decline is being accelerated by hunting for trade.

If the destruction of the planet continues at the present rate, the effects will be as disastrous as that of a nuclear war. However, we have been warned. Chief Seattle, a native American who lived between 1788 and 1866, said to his people:

'Man did not weave the web of life.
He's merely a strand of it.
Whatever he does to the web of life he does to himself.'

If we, the people of the earth, are to resolve the crises which threaten our environment and human life, we must be properly informed so that we can take suitable action. We need to recognise that we must live in harmony with other forms of life to maintain the environments which we need to survive.

There have already been some conservation successes. Changes in the disposal of chemicals have enabled some animals and fish to return in numbers to rivers in many developed countries. Also, the conscious protection of many species and their environments by government agencies or environmental lobbies has led to the reintroduction of animals in to the wild from captive breeding programmes.

The activities in this book aim to help children understand the meaning of the words of Chief Seattle, i.e. the direct relationship between human action and the state of the global environment. Many of these activities focus on what children could do to help improve their local environment. However, the aim is also to raise their awareness of the status of many different types of habitat, and the conservation issues which relate to them.

Wherever possible, the children's own knowledge or experience of conservation issues or campaigns should be used. They may be able to give valuable information about conservation initiatives which are taking place in the local area or at a national level. Encourage them to become involved as a class or as individuals.

The Rainforest - Ideas Page

Aims

- To introduce the concept and characteristics of rainforest layers. Each layer is the habitat for a variety of species.
- For children to experience an environment different from their own, by simulating rainforest conditions.

Background

Tropical rainforests are found in a narrow belt close to the equator, in Africa, Asia, South and Central America. Although they account for only 2% of the earth's surface, they play a vital role in the biosphere, absorbing harmful carbon dioxide gases and supplying oxygen. Rainforests also affect weather conditions, and the air we breathe, as well as being home to thousands of specialised species of plants and animals. It has been estimated that by AD2000 over 80% of rainforests will have been destroyed, unless problems of over population and the demand for lumber are resolved.

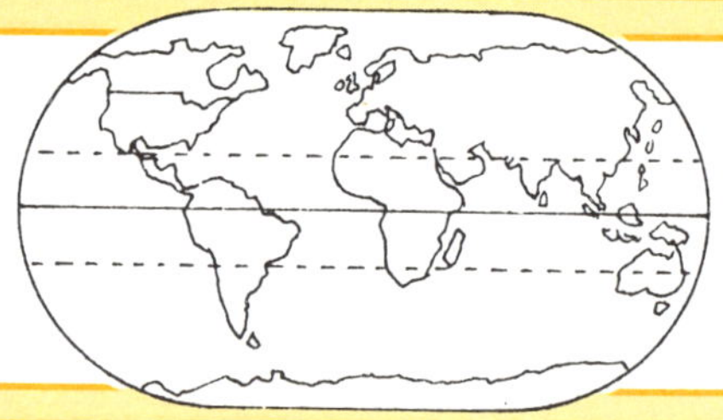

Activities

- Begin by locating areas of rainforest on a world map. Then talk about the animals shown on the activity sheet. Children may already be familiar with similar species. Ask children to match the animals to the correct rainforest layers. Provide them with appropriate reference material to complete the task.
- Children could find out about the behaviour of these rainforest animals. Talk about how they have adapted to their environment:
  - How do they move?
  - What do they feed on?
  - Do they like light?

- Create a rainforest environment in class. Hang some shower curtains in a corner and fill the space with a variety of plants. Place large pans of steaming water on the floor inside the area, and wait. Allow children to go into the 'forest'. Talk about the difference between the humidity and temperature in the forest area and the rest of the classroom. What is happening to the sides of the curtains?

Developments

- Make a rainforest mobile to reinforce any new vocabulary. Copy new words from the activity sheet on to cards. Suspend them from wire hangers or dowel along with animals cut or copied from the sheet.

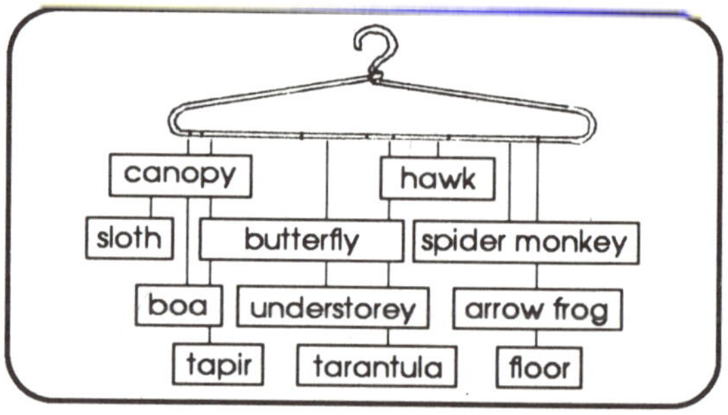

- Design and make exotic rainforest creatures, e.g. giant butterflies. Cut large shapes from black paper, and create stained glass window effects on the wings using coloured tissue paper. Suspend these in the rainforest area.
- Provide groups of children with copies of the activity sheet. Brainstorm words relating to the rainforest layers, e.g. high, tall, leafy, sunny, canopy. Children could use these words to write poems about each layer. Staple the work together as a huge class concertina book entitled 'Our Book of the Rainforest'.

The Rainforest

- Match the animals to the correct rainforest layers.
- Find out why they live in these layers.

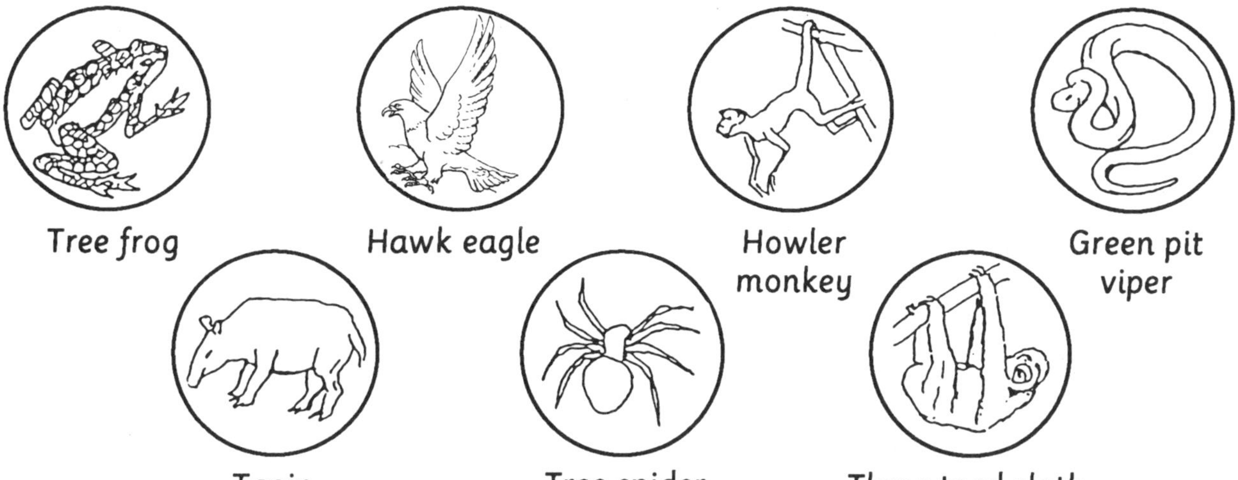

Disappearing Rainforests - *Ideas Page*

Aim

- To consolidate children's knowledge of rainforests - their location, vegetation, vegetation strata and growth.

Background

Rainforests are found in a narrow belt close to the equator, in Africa, Asia, South and Central America. They are essential to our lives, as they absorb carbon dioxide and give off oxygen. Cutting down large areas of rainforest will affect the climate and the air we breathe.
Rainforests are made up of four distinct layers of vegetation: emergent trees, the canopy, understorey and herb layer. Each is the habitat for a plant and animal community.

Activities

- Identify the listed areas of rainforest on the world map provided.
- Make a rainforest model, by using: a breakfast cereal box 27cm high or higher, three cardboard tubes 23cm high, e.g. kitchen paper tubes, three tubes 12cm high, e.g. toilet tissue tubes, modelling clay, drawing paper, scissors and coloured pencils. (The diagram will help you.) Use the model to discuss the characteristics of the vegetation layers.

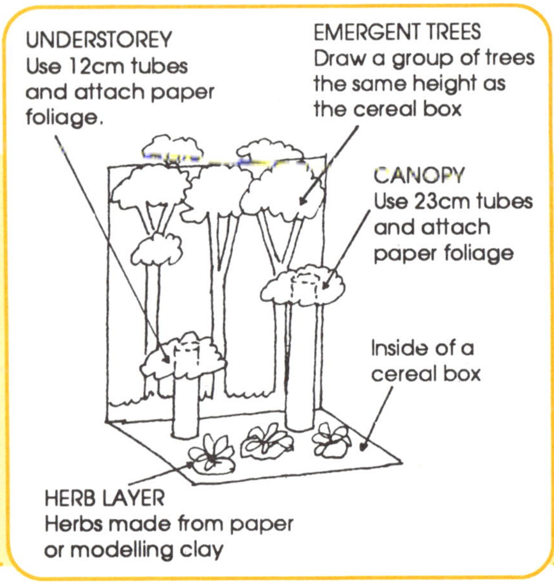

- Make a mini rainforest in an aquarium, using some gravel and charcoal, compost, a few stones and some house plants. Cover the aquarium with glass or plastic and keep out of direct sunlight. Ask the children why the 'rainforest' requires so little water to survive. What do they notice about the temperature of this environment when they place their hands inside the aquarium?

Developments

- Increase children's awareness of the economic factors which may lead to the destruction of rainforests. Children could find out where different types of wood come from.
  - Why are people cutting down large areas of tropical rainforest when there are supplies of wood elsewhere?
  - What is special about this wood?

  Introduce the idea of living resources, and the conflicting demands of consumers and producers, e.g. of a farmer and a manufacturer.
- Provide the children with a copy of table **A**. Ask them which of the countries is losing most forest land each year. Why do they think this is happening?
- Locate the countries listed in **A** on a blank map of the world. The children could draw bar charts to display the data. What does the data tell them about what is happening to rainforests worldwide? Talk about the wider implications of this destruction, e.g. the threat to the indigenous populations of these areas.

A

Countries	Millions of acres lost each year	% of total land lost
Brazil	8.5	0.7
Indonesia	3.0	1.0
Bolivia	2.5	2.1
Mexico	2.3	1.9
Venezuela	2.1	1.5
Zaire	1.8	0.6
Peru	1.4	0.9
Burma	1.2	1.6
Malaysia	0.9	2.0

Tropical Rainforests

- Mark on the world map:
  the Equator
  the Tropic of Cancer
  the Tropic of Capricorn
  the Continents
  the Oceans.

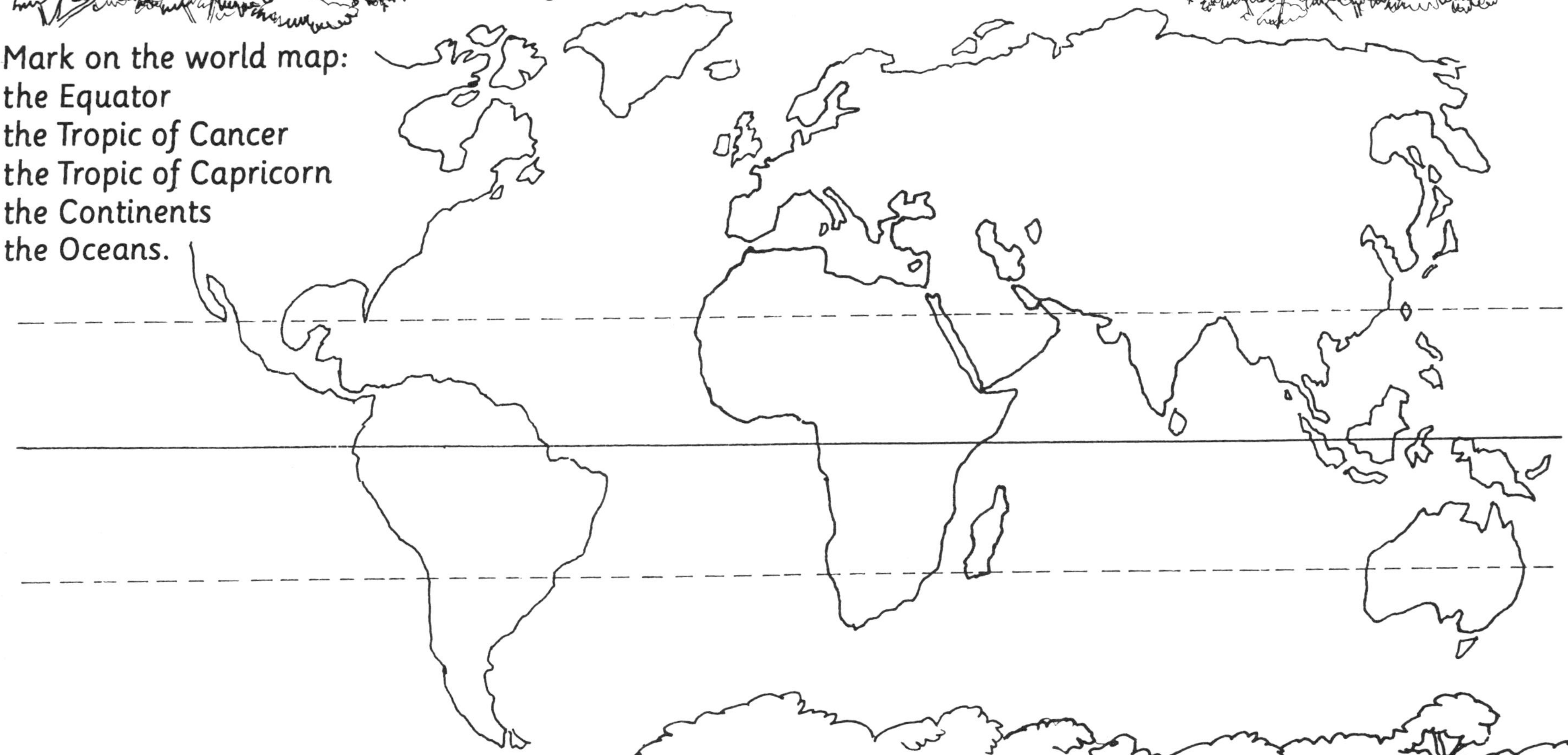

Even though more than 40% of the rainforests have been destroyed, there are still large areas of rainforest in:

Congo	Ghana	Guinea	Malaysia	Sri Lanka	Equador
Madagascar	Nigeria	Indonesia	Thailand	Brazil	Guatemala.

NOW

- Find and mark these countries on the map.
- Colour the areas of rainforest.

Biomes - Ideas Page

Aims

- To familiarise children with ecological regions.
- To increase their awareness of the threats to these environments.

Background

Seventy percent of our planet is water. From space it looks blue, so it is known as the 'Blue Planet'.
There are fifteen major ecological regions or 'biomes' which cover the earth. Each has a different combination of climatic conditions, rock and soil types, water resources and latitude. As a result they support different types of animal and plant life. All this life exists in the biosphere - the life layer. This stretches from the deepest part of the ocean to 15km above the earth's surface.

Activities

- Provide children with appropriate reference material to complete the activity, including atlases. Children who have chosen the same biome to research should compare their results, to show how elements of the same type of ecological region may differ.
- Children who have researched different biomes should form into groups to talk about their results.
- After the class have completed their research on a country within a biome, ask them to write a newspaper report or devise a TV feature on their area and its plant and animal community, e.g.

In this hot rainforest area, it rains a lot - up to 8 metres a year! Tropical rainforests are being chopped down for human needs. The homes of many animals like the mountain gorillas in Africa are disappearing.

Developments

- Demonstrate how to work out the relative area of the land compared with the sea. Trace areas of land and sea from a world map. Cut out the areas of land and paste them together on a piece of squared paper. Do the same for the sea. Then calculate the percentage of water and land in relation to the total area.
- Children could draw a bar chart to show the percentages of each land type on the 'Blue Planet'.

Land	Amount
Desert	33%
Permanent ice	11%
Frozen land	10%
Left to use	46%

NB. 'Frozen land' will thaw out.

Encourage children to analyse the data by asking these questions:
- What is the land actually used for?
- Why is it difficult to use some of these areas?

- Prepare and provide the children with two outline maps of the world. Label them:
  - 1 000 years ago
  - Now.

  Explain that 1 000 years ago half of the world was covered by forest. Locate this area and shade it. (Africa below the Sahara and above South Africa, Europe, the Far East, Sri Lanka, Bangladesh, Malaysia, Oceania and Western Australia.) Now only one fifth of the world is covered by forest. Colour the areas of tropical rainforests and the few temperate forests of North America, Australia, Europe and South America. Ask the children to suggest reasons why the natural vegetation of these areas has changed over time.

Biomes

A biome is a part of the world where only certain types of plants and animals live. Each biome has its own type of climate and landscape.

Below are five of the world's biomes:

Tundra and ice	Forest	Desert	Grassland	Rainforest

- Choose one of these. Use an atlas to find out which parts of the world are in this biome. Mark these areas on the map below and design a suitable key.

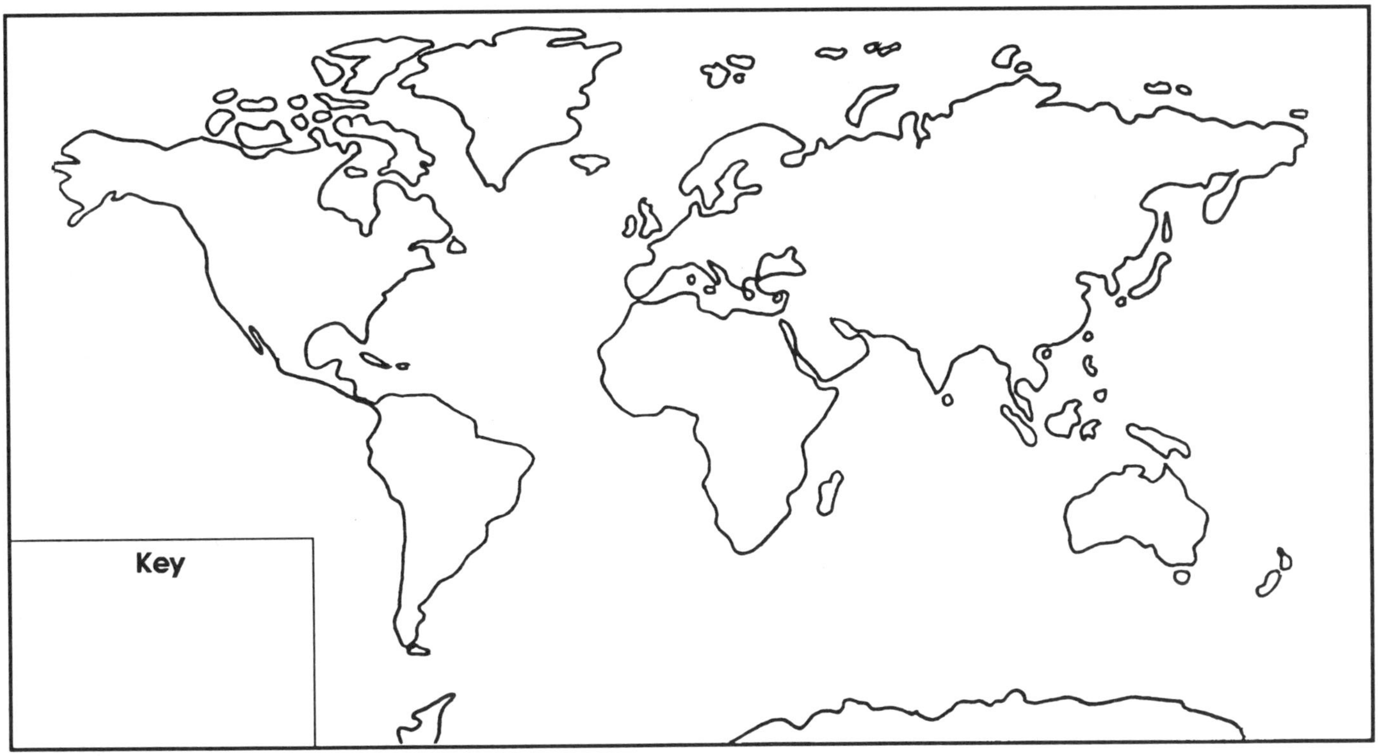

NOW

- Choose one country in your biome.
  Carry out some research and complete the table.

Vegetation	Climate	Plants and animals	Conservation issue

Continue over the page.

Animals in Danger - Ideas Page

Aim

- To highlight the work being carried out by zoos worldwide to help animals under threat of extinction.
- To increase children's awareness of endangered animals in their own country.

Activities

Answers:

1 = Giant panda from China
2 = Black rhino from Africa
3 = Indian tiger from India and South East Asia
4 = Przewalski's horse
5 = African elephant from Kenya, Africa
6 = Duck-billed platypus from Australasia.

- All the animals listed above are facing extinction because their habitat is being destroyed by humans. Children could research one of these animals to find out why it is under threat. Suggest that they plan a campaign to save the animal. It may be useful for the teacher to collect a range of conservation leaflets to be used as a class resource.
- Explain the term 'extinction'. It means that no more of a species is left. Children should be made aware that extinction is forever. 'Endangered' means that the numbers of a type of animal are falling, and their kind could disappear if no action is taken.

Background

Animals are becoming extinct because their habitats are being destroyed - the places where they live, eat and breed. The causes of this are:
- humans clearing land
- humans hunting the animals
- animals being killed illegally
- competition between species, as in the case of the red and grey squirrel.

Zoos around the world keep records of animals in captivity, and in some cases they count animal populations in the wild, so that they can take action if a species is under threat.

Developments

- Find out about the work of the following organisations:
  - The Worldwide Fund for Nature (WWF)
  - The Zoological Society of London
  - The Jersey Conservation Trust.
- Some species which were common until very recently are now under threat:
  - There are 25% fewer robins today than there were twenty years ago.
  - Red squirrels are only found in a few parts of northern England.
  - Frogs and certain kinds of toads are protected animals in England.

  Children could find out which species are under threat in their local area. Local wildlife trusts may be able to provide details of their initiatives.
- Children could draw bar charts to show the data below:

Numbers in existence

Black rhino	
1970	1 500
1980	1 000
Most recent	400

African elephant	
1970	1.3 million
1980	764 000
Most recent	650 000

Sea turtles	
1970	2 000
1980	700
Most recent	600

- Use these questions to discuss the endangered animals:
  - What is happening in all three cases?
  - Why are the numbers decreasing?
  - What could be done to increase the numbers of these species?

Animals in Danger

This page shows some animals which are close to extinction.

Name: ____________ Name: ____________ Name: ____________

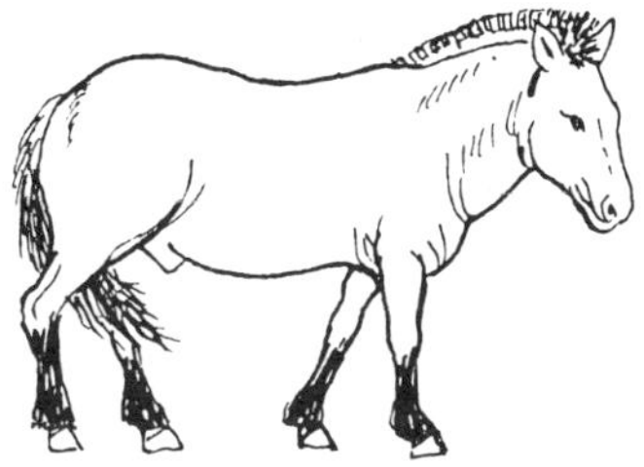

Name: ____________ Name: ____________ Name: ____________

- Find out the names of the animals and write them in the spaces.
- Research one of the animals and fill in the chart below.

Animal	Where it comes from	Reasons for being in danger

NOW
- Think about how you could help to save one of these animals. Plan a campaign.

Stop the Trade - Ideas Page

Aim

- To explain that many animals are killed for commercial reasons. Most of the killing is illegal and is carried out by poachers.

Background

The international trade in wildlife and animal products is big business. In 1991, this industry made about ten billion (10 000 000 000) pounds; three quarters of this profit was earned illegally. It is this illegal trade which is endangering many species of plants and animals.
In some countries, animals are farmed for particular products, e.g. crocodiles in Zimbabwe. This is one way to save endangered animals from extinction.

Activities

Answers:
Dagger handle = Rhino
Umbrella stand = Elephant
Wall ornament = Turtle
Handbag = Crocodile
Shoes = Lizard
Coat = Leopard
Drum skin = Zebra
Rug = Tiger.

- Talk about the objects on the activity sheet:
  - What do the children think they are used for?
  - Where do they come from?
  - Why do people want to buy these goods?
  - Would they want them so much if they knew exactly where they came from and the problems they were causing?
- Use an atlas to point out the countries of origin of the items.
- Talk about how these products are transported, e.g. smuggling by individuals or large companies.

Developments

In 1986, 6-700 000 live parrots were caught and sent to other countries.

- Provide children with an outline map of the world. Ask them to find and mark the top exporters of parrots: Argentina, Tanzania, Indonesia, Germany, Guyana. Then they should mark the top importers: United States, Germany, UK, Netherlands and Japan. What do they notice? (Germany is in both lists) Why should this be? What is happening to the parrots once they reach Germany? Children could find out what these animals are used for. They may need to contact a local or national conservation group.
- Ask children which animals provide ivory:
  - Where do they come from?
  - What is ivory used for?
  - Why do people like to own it?
  - Do elephants have to be killed for their ivory?
  - Why do the children think that there is a world ban on ivory imports?
- Do children think there is a difference between trading in live animals and trading in goods from these animals?
- Draw symbols for each kind of import in **A**. Children could find out where these animals come from. Paste the symbols on to a chart or a map of the world with these figures for imports (1986).

A

Goods imported	Number imported
Live chimps and apes	51 000
Cat skins	192 000
Reptile skins	10 481 000
Ivory	43 000

NB. A world ban has now reduced the trade.

- Ask each child to choose an animal from the table of imports (above), and to find out what happens to the animal and its products.
- How could children 'Stop the Trade'? Groups of children could develop a strategy to save one of the animals.

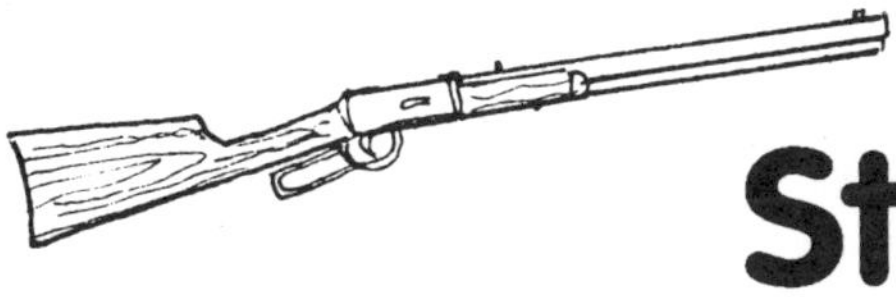

Stop the Trade

All the objects in the boxes have been made from animals.

- Match each object to the correct animal.

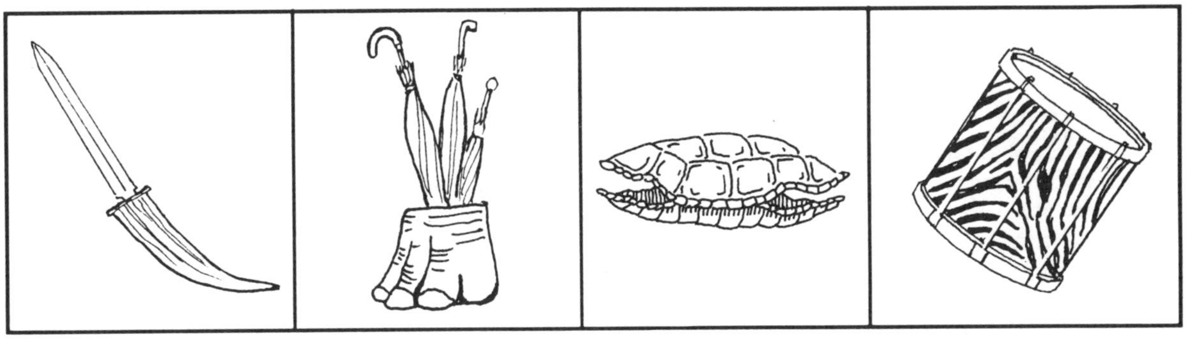

Name of object: ________ ________ ________ ________

Animal: ________ ________ ________ ________

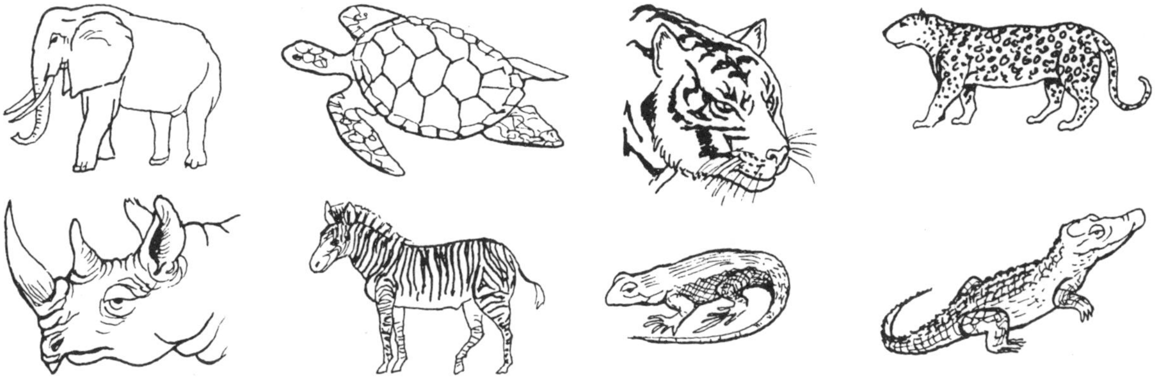

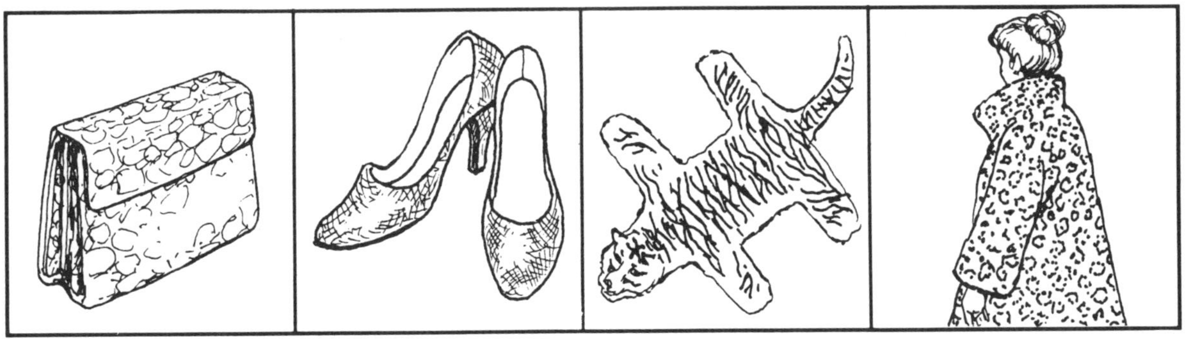

Name of object: ________ ________ ________ ________

Animal: ________ ________ ________ ________

NOW

- Talk about what could be done to stop the trade in wildlife products.

Whales - Ideas Page

Aim

- To increase children's knowledge and understanding of whales and whaling.

Activities

Answers:
- The three main whale products are meat, bone and oil.
- These are used in the manufacture of common household products, e.g. pet food and soap.

- Children will need to be provided with appropriate reference material or given access to a library, to complete their research on whales.
- Talk about the figures for whales hunted in 1987.

Number of whales caught in 1987:	
Japan	**2 245**
Russia	**3 028**
Norway	**373**
Greenland	**90**

Encourage children to examine the data by asking questions, such as:
- How many whales were hunted in this year?
- Who hunted the most whales?

Extend the activity by suggesting children find out where whaling takes place. They could then mark these areas on a world map.

Background

There are a wide variety of whale species: the baleen whales (blue whales, the longest animals on earth, the humpback and bowhead whales) and the toothed whales (sperm whales, white whales, dolphins and porpoises).
Whales have no natural enemies except human beings. They are easy prey for hunters because they are air breathers. Whalers follow them, wait until they surface for a breath, then kill them.
Whales have been hunted for many centuries for their products. Whale bone used to be made into corsets for fashionable Western ladies. Today, whale oil and meat are the most important products.

Developments

- The blue whale is the largest animal to have ever lived. Encourage children to find out more about it.
- Talk about famous whale stories, e.g. Jonah and the Whale, Moby Dick. What types of whales are represented in these stories? How are they portrayed - as evil creatures wanting to harm humans?
- Dolphins and porpoises are whales too, and they are also hunted for their products. Children could research their behaviour. What experiences do the children have of these animals through TV programmes and books? Were they surprised to find out that these animals are types of whales?
- When whales give birth the baby is born 'breech', i.e. tail first, and a 'nurse' whale is in attendance to push the baby to the surface. Why is this an important piece of behaviour?
- When whales are stranded or 'beached' they are helpless, and yet in the water they are graceful movers, rushing effortlessly through the water. Are the children able to explain this? The following experiment aims to help children to understand this phenomenon.
  Make 'whales' from modelling clay. Weigh them using a force metre spring balance on 'land' and then in water. What do the children notice? Explain that water provides an upthrust which is exerted in the opposite direction to the pull of gravity. This means that in water the whale's large mass is not an impediment. Stranded on land, it has to support its own mass and is therefore unable to move.

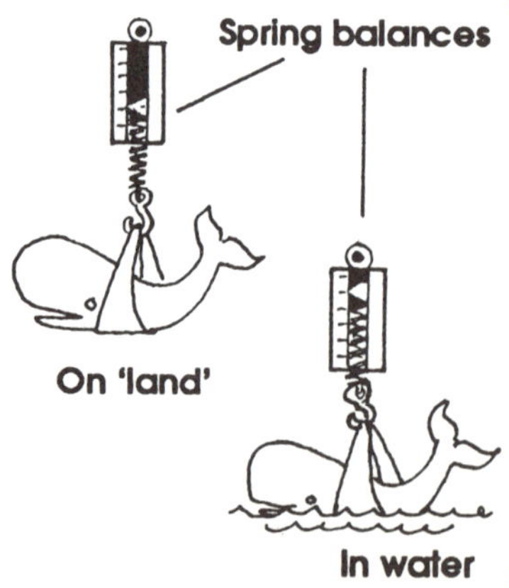

Whales

- Find out which parts of the whale humans use.
- Write these on the whale below.

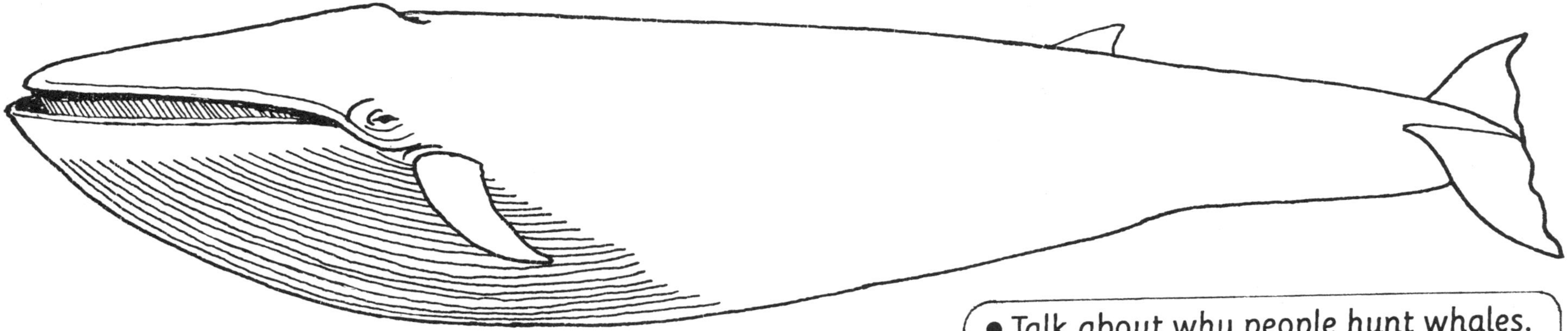

NOW • Complete the chart.

Whale product	Used for

- Talk about why people hunt whales.
- Could we obtain the products in any other way?
- What could be done to make sure that whales do not become extinct?

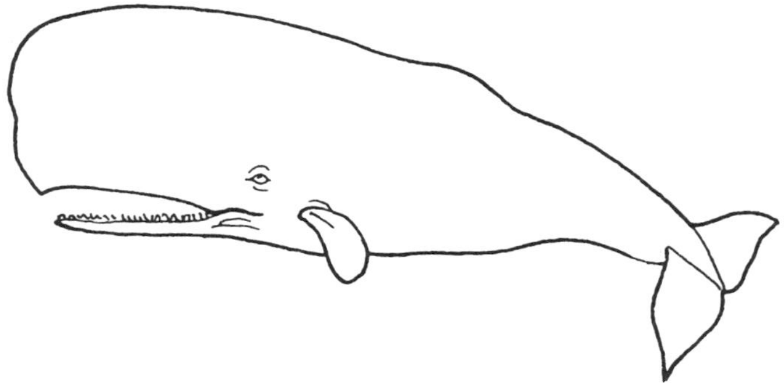

Plants in Danger - Ideas Page

Aim

- To introduce children to some issues affecting plant habitats, and the debate between bio-conservationists, farmers and planners.

Activities

- Use the examples on the activity sheet to discuss the factors which threaten plant species. Their habitat is either:
  - being destroyed by developers
  - changed because of new agricultural methods
  - altered because of new activities, e.g. tourism.
- Before the children write their newspaper report, ask groups to act out one of the situations.

- Ask children what happens if wild flowers are picked. Where do the seeds go? Will new plants grow from these seeds? After carrying out research, children may be able to suggest ways in which wild flowers could be conserved.

Developments

- Children could role play, e.g. the 'Twyford Downs situation', to learn more about the conflicting views which arise when a local habitat is under threat. The following ideas may be used to simulate local conservation debates.
- Children could take the following roles:
  - A local leader, who explains the situation to people from the surrounding area, e.g. how the road could improve access to the area, or cause excessive noise and pollution.
  - A local natural history expert, who wants people to know about the plight of the orchids.
  - Local people giving their opinions.
  - Reporters, who listen and record the main points of the argument, e.g. is the road needed or could planners use an alternative route?
- Ask the reporters to read out their lists. Then the local people summarise their viewpoints. Use this information as the basis for a class discussion of the situation. This is a suitable time for the children to write their reports.

Speaker	Point of view
Local farmer	1. would cause noise pollution and spoil the milk of his cows. 2. would destroy the beauty of the local area

- Once the reports are written, continue the simulation. Elect children to play the role of the official planner and some of the townspeople. Suggest they explain their side of the argument, e.g. roads are clogged with traffic trying to travel from London to the South West on holiday and on business.
- What do the children think of these points of view? Have they changed their minds about the project?
- Britain is home to 70% of all mosses and liverwort in Europe. 209 of these European lichens are threatened species. Why do the children think they are safer on an island? Children could find out about mosses and liverwort - their habitats and life cycles.

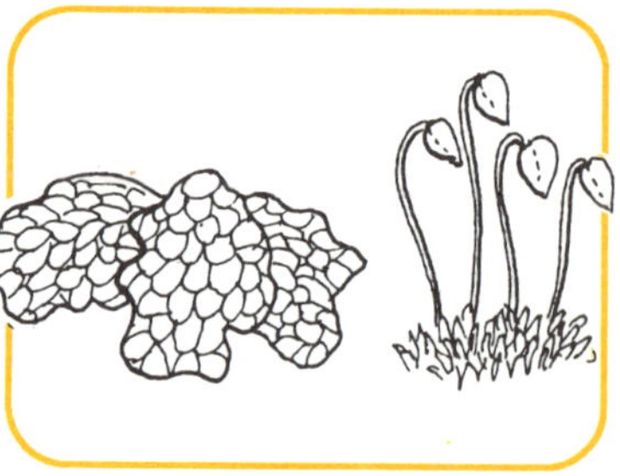

- Ask groups of children to design a logo for Britain as the moss/liverwort refuge. They could include a short message or slogan. Children may find it helpful to refer to a range of conservation leaflets.

Plants in Danger

- Study the map carefully. It shows some areas where plants are under threat.

CAIRNGORMS
The winter sports industry is destroying this habitat.

WELSH PEATBOG
Many rare peat plants and eighteen different types of dragonfly will disappear if people build on this land.

THE FENS
This area is drying out as farmers change the way they farm.

NORFOLK BROADS
Pollution is causing water lilies to disappear.

TWYFORD DOWN
The building of the Winchester by-pass has destroyed the homes of six different types of orchids and that of the rare blue chalk fritillary butterfly.

- Imagine you are a reporter living near one of these areas. Write an article to show how local people feel about the destruction of plants' homes.

School Times

Plants in Danger

____

____

____

____

____

______________________ Continue over the page.

Wildlife Conservation - Ideas Page

Aim

- To raise the children's awareness of wildlife conservation issues: what the messages are, where they can send messages, receive responses and action them.

Activities

- If designing a T-shirt is too difficult, then make badges. Badges could be made from card circles with a safety pin attached. Before each child designs their badge or T-shirt ask him/her:
  - What is the purpose of the badge/T-shirt?
  - What message do they wish to communicate?
  - What will the picture 'say'?
  - What will the words 'say'?
- Provide children with ideas for logo designs, e.g. charity emblems collected from advertisements and brochures.

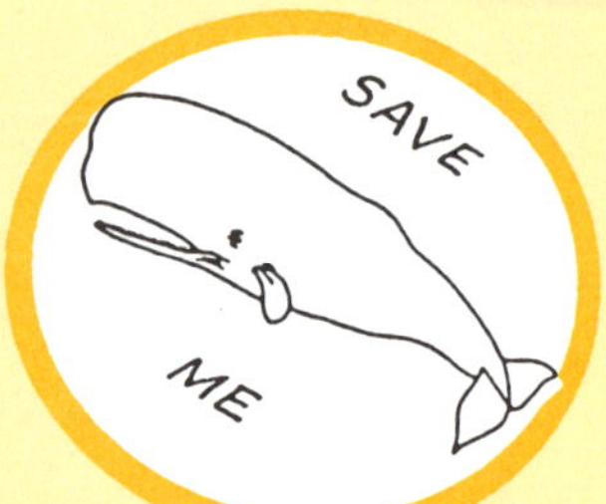

Background

Communication is about getting a message across to people. Before starting the T-shirt/badge-making activity, remember to tell the children:

- that the fewer words they use the better
- to use distinctive symbols
- to be different
- to be uncluttered
- to make the visual instantly recognisable.

Children could use ideas from conservation projects that they are familiar with, e.g. 'Save the Panda' and 'Save the Whale'. It is important for children to realise that wildlife conservation is not something which happens a long way away in other countries.

Conservation is about:

- preventing habitats from disappearing or being so altered that species cannot adapt to the changes
- reintroducing healthy animals and plants to places where they used to live, if these areas are safe
- keeping healthy plants and animals alive in captivity so that species do not become extinct.

Developments

- Prepare a class project on conservation. Children could choose an endangered animal and work through the 'conservation' points in the background section, offering solutions to their animal's particular problems.
- Barn owls are endangered because their habitats are disappearing. Children could find out where they live. Why are these places disappearing? What could children do to help?
- Many insects are attracted to certain plants. What kinds of plants attract butterflies? Why? Are these the same types of plants which attract other insects, e.g. bees?

	No. of butterflies
Daisy	𝍸 II
Buttercup	III

- Plant a butterfly garden. Children could keep a visual diary to show how many kinds of butterfly visit the garden, and when.

Wildlife Conservation

- Design a logo for the front of this T-shirt which promotes a conservation issue.

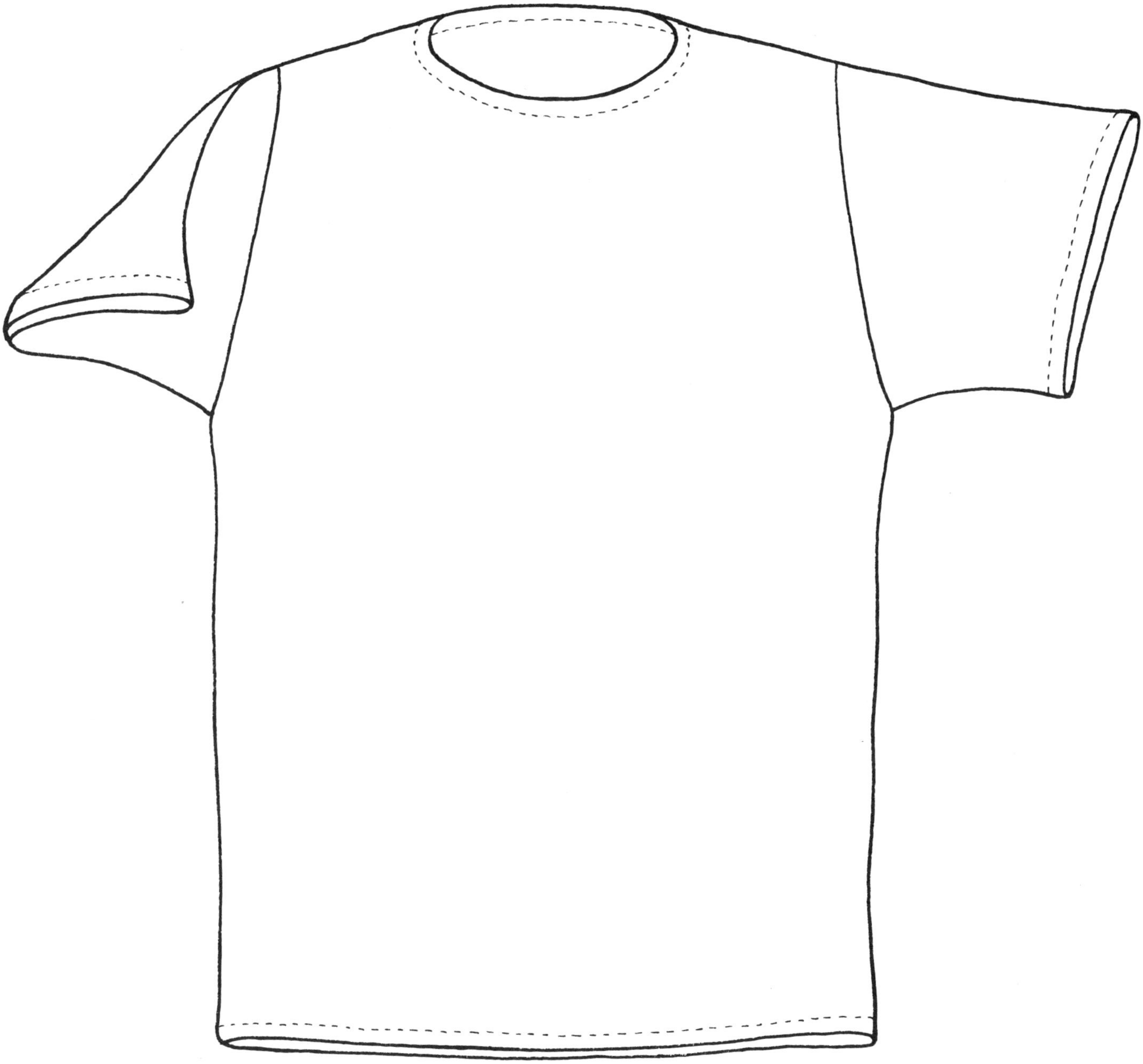

- How will you transfer your design to a real shirt?
- Make your T-shirt and wear it. Do people notice the logo? What do they say?

The Population Riddle - Ideas Page

Aim

- To increase children's awareness of the rapid growth of the world's population, who will all need a share in the earth's resources. These resources are finite.

Background

The world population is 5.3 billion (5 300 000 000), with 250 000 more babies being born each day (90 million a year). The population is unevenly distributed throughout the world.

Activities

- The children should be reminded that if couples had only two babies each and these survived, the population would remain the same - a zero growth rate.
  Once people do more than replace themselves the population increases.

Generation 1:
2 people have 4 babies: 4 - 2 (the parents) = an increase of 2.
Generation 2:
The 4 children have 16 babies: the net increase is 16 - 8 (parents) = 8.
Generation 3:
16 children have 4 babies each = 64. 64 - 32 (parents 16 x 2) = a population increase of 32.
Generation 4:
These 64 children, if they have 4 babies each, produce 256 babies, but as each family has 2 parents this is 128 adults. Therefore, there are 128 more people.

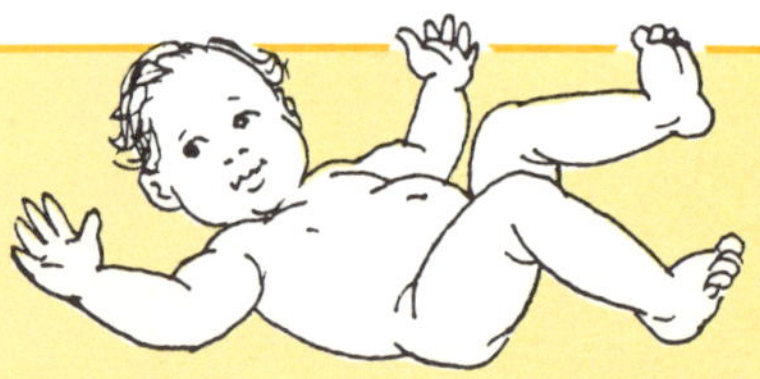

Developments

- Provide children with a copy of the list of cities (**A**) and an outline map of the world. Children will need to use an atlas to locate and mark the cities on their map. This could be entitled 'AD2000 - the World's Largest Cities'.

A The World's Largest Cities in AD2000

City	Projected population in millions
Mexico City	25.8
Rio de Janeiro	13.3
Tokyo	20.2
Bombay	16.0
Seoul	13.8
Tehran	13.6
Sao Paulo	24.0
Calcutta	16.5
New York	15.8
Shanghai	14.3

- Children could rank the cities in decreasing size and draw a block graph to show the data. Suggest that they make a three-dimensional representation of this information from boxes or tubes. 1cm to 1 million people is a suitable scale. The children could find the present populations of the cities and do the same. What do they notice? Why are certain cities growing faster than others?
- Alternatively, display a map of the world on a table and arrange appropriately sized tubes, with the city's name written on one side and the population size on the other.
- Discuss the data in **A**. Which areas of the world have the most populated cities? Which are in 'poorer' countries? Are the two factors related?
- Encourage children to think about the action cities will have to take as their populations expand, so that people:
  - live a healthy life
  - are able to buy food
  - have somewhere to live and sleep
  - have enough money to pay for all of these things.

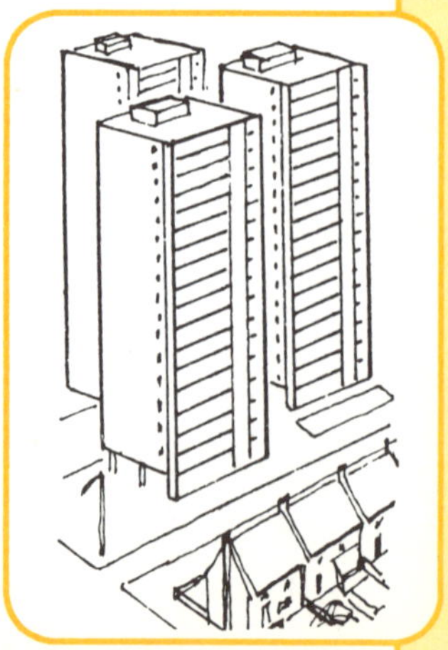

The Population Riddle

If every couple in the world has four children, and every child has four children, how many children will there be by the fourth generation?

- *Draw a family tree to find out. You may need a very large sheet of paper!*

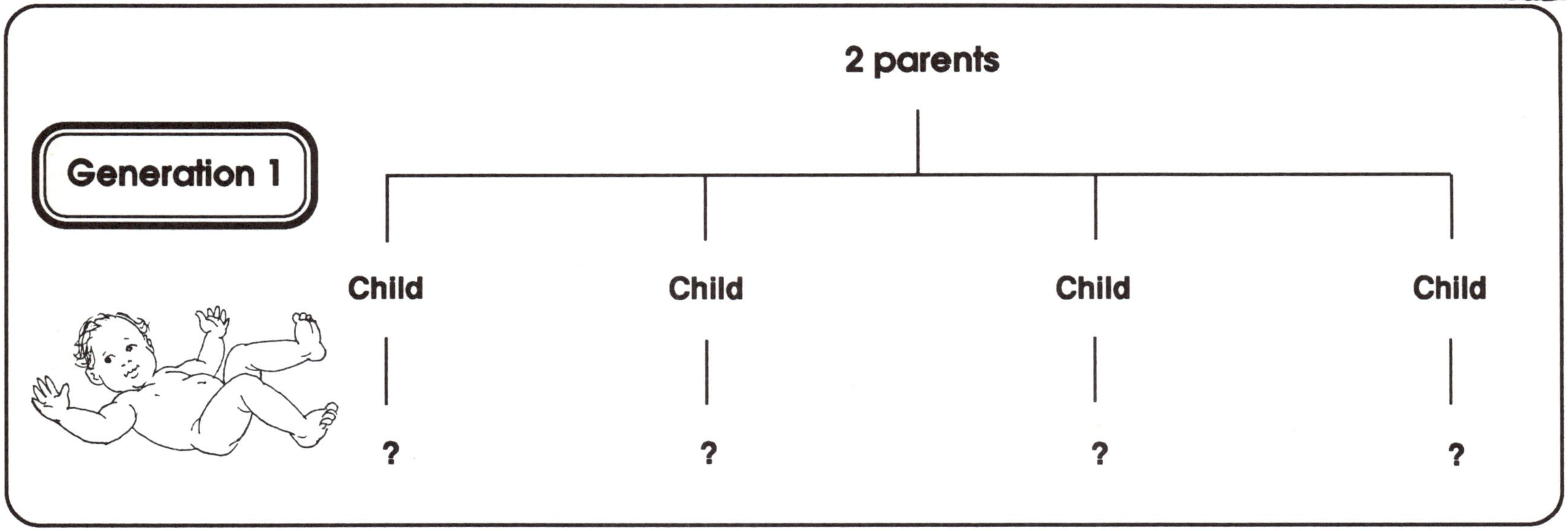

Fact File

Today, there are 5 300 000 thousand people in the world. Each day 250 000 more are born. Scientists expect there to be 8 000 000 thousand people on earth by 2025, and 14 000 000 thousand by 2100.

- Draw a bar chart to show how the world's population will grow from now to 2100.
- *Talk about what might happen in 2100. Where will all the people live? What will they eat?*

Clean Water - Ideas Page

Aims

- To teach children about the water cycle.
- To examine environmental issues associated with clean water.

Activities

- The pollution card 'fits' in several places:
  - Nitrates infiltrate the land and water, so animals and plants become contaminated and some may die.
  - Rainwater washes nitrates from the land into lakes, seas and rivers. These encourage algae to grow. When the algae die they rot, using up oxygen in the water. This causes fish and plants to die.

  Many nitrates remain active for hundreds of years, continuing to damage the environment.

A

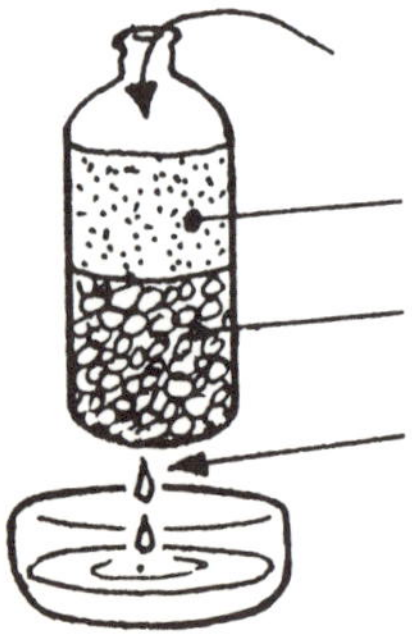

Developments

- With so 'little' water available, it is a precious commodity. Conduct a water audit. Children could write down everything they use water for. Can they think of any alternatives to using water?
- Conduct a class survey to see how much water could be saved during a week:
  - How much water is used if the tap is left running while children brush their teeth?
  - How much water would be saved if they used only one glass full?
  - How much water is saved by having a shower instead of a bath?
- List practical ways of saving water in the school and at home. Suggest that the children try some of these. Are they difficult to implement?
- Make a model to explain the concept of condensation, from: plastic wrap (cling film), modelling clay, a transparent container, water and tape. Set up the equipment in a sunny place. What do the children think might happen? The water will evaporate, condense and collect in drops on the film. These will eventually fall back into the dish.

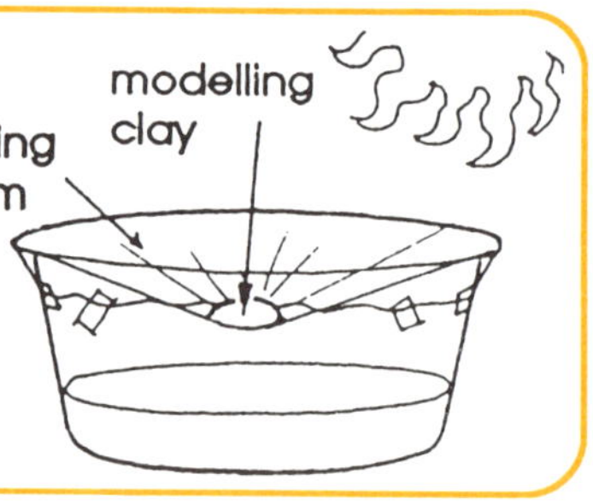

- Not all people in the world have access to clean water. How could a sample of clean water be obtained?

  Mix soil and water together in a pot. Leave the pot to stand. What happens? Strain the water through a piece of kitchen towel. What happens?
- Waterworks clean water by filtering it through sand and pebbles. Children could make a similar type of filter. Provide them with plastic containers (e.g. cut down 500ml soft drinks bottles). Demonstrate how to make a filter:
  - Make a hole in the base of a plastic container.
  - Place a layer of pebbles at the bottom, and a layer of sand on top.
  - Pour dirty water in at the top of the filter and collect it in a small bowl at the bottom, as shown in **A**.

  Children could record their observations of the experiment.

Clean Water

- The cards below describe the different parts of the water cycle. Cut them out and place them in the correct order.

Some water collects in surface or underground lakes.

When clouds meet a cold air mass, large droplets of water form. These fall to the earth as rain or snow, and drain via rivers into the sea.

Clouds are evaporated water. Water vapour rises, cools, and forms clouds (tiny droplets of water).

Plants collect water from the soil through their roots.

The sun heats the water from the land, sea, and from plants. This evaporates into the air.

- Add the pollution card to your cycle. What effect would it have on the environment?

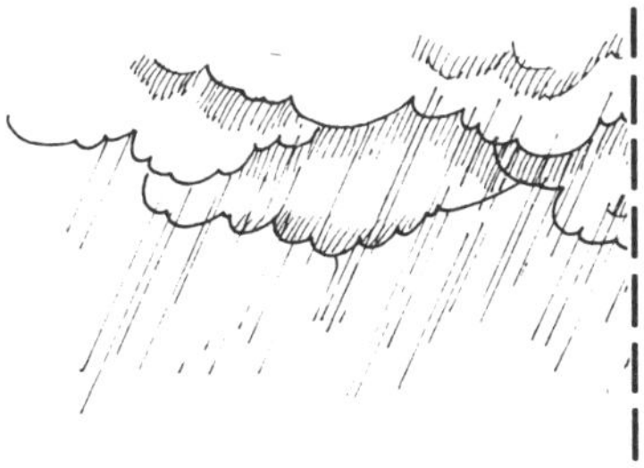

POLLUTION IN THE SOIL OR WATER.
This could be nitrates from fertilizers or chemicals from factories.

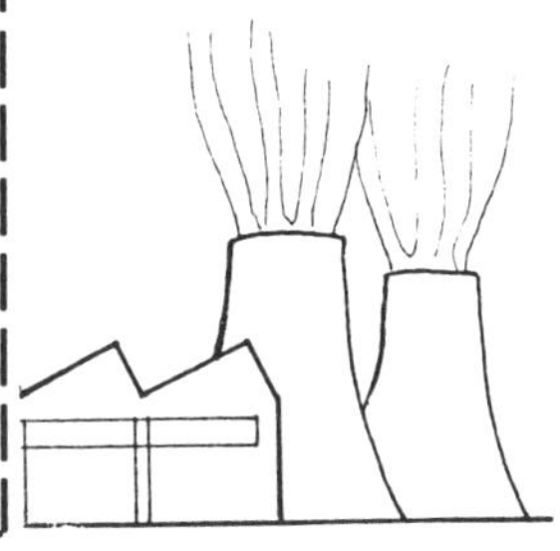

Air Pollution - Ideas Page

Aim

- To explain that the air around us is part of the environment and, as such, is at risk from pollution.

Activities

- Set the scene for a discussion on air pollution. Ask the children what air is, where it is and what is in it.
- Suggest that children design and make paper fans. Encourage them to waft the fans in front of their faces, to feel the moving air.
- Does moving air have anything in it? Children could look through a beam of sunlight or the beam from a slide projector to see dust particles in the air.
- Collect some newspapers for the class to read, and cut out articles which refer to air pollution. Then make notes from the articles:
  - What are the main pollutants?
  - Are the Clean Air Acts mentioned?
- Encourage children to find out about the fogs in London during the 1950s. What caused them, and how were they eradicated? The Clean Air Acts have had a remarkable effect. We are now moving away from coal fuels. What are we using instead? Do these fuels create any environmental problems?

Background

The main air pollutants and where they come from are summarised in this table:

Pollutant	Source
Sulphur dioxide	Power stations
Nitrogen dioxide	Incineration
Hydrocarbons	Old refineries, vehicle exhaust fumes
Carbon monoxide	Vehicle fumes, industries, heavy metals
Organic chemicals	Chemical industries.

Once in the air, these pollutants react with each other to form deadly chemicals, e.g. acid rain.

Developments

A 'pollutant' catcher

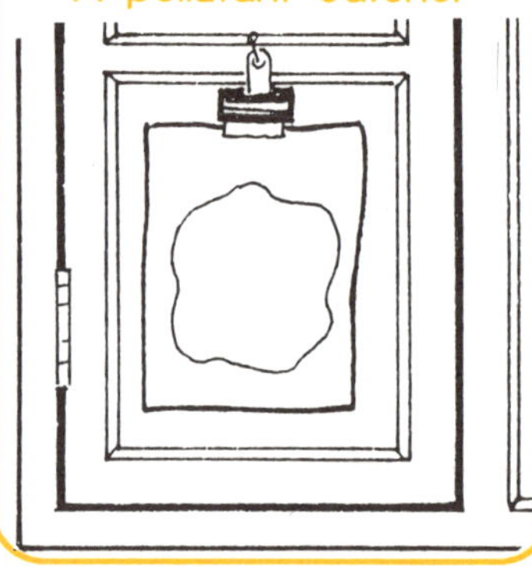

- Children could design a test to find out if there is anything else in the air. Carry out this experiment to discover whether the content of air varies in different locations. For this experiment use: pieces of filter paper or sugar paper, scissors, petroleum jelly, bulldog or paper clips, lollipop sticks or cotton buds.
- To make this a fair test, each piece of card should be the same size, and the same amount of jelly should be smeared over the same sized area.
- Children could plan where they are going to place the 'pollutant' catchers, and position them, e.g. high up in class, at floor level or head level, by the school gate, in the corridor, by a window.
- A control 'pollutant' measure should be placed inside a sealed polythene box to use as a reference point.
- Decide how long the catchers will be left in place. Then take them down to see which has caught the most particles, i.e. changed colour.
- The children could design a scale - the control being 0, and draw a bar graph for the results of the experiment.

- Are there any buildings in the immediate environment which have had their features etched away by air pollution? Discuss why this corrosion takes place, and how it may be prevented.

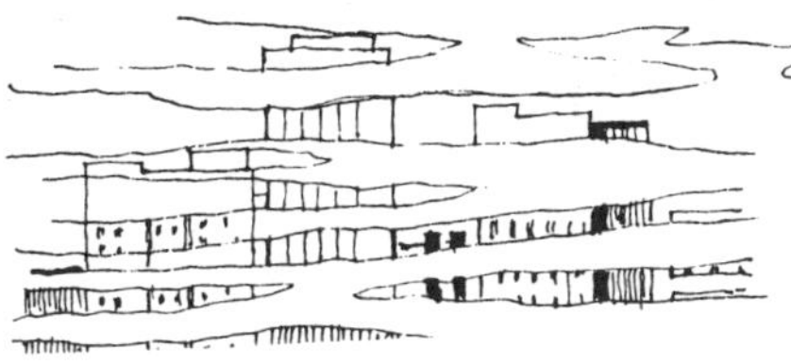

Air Pollution

In many parts of the world the air is very polluted.

- Find the places described in the news headlines and mark them on the map.

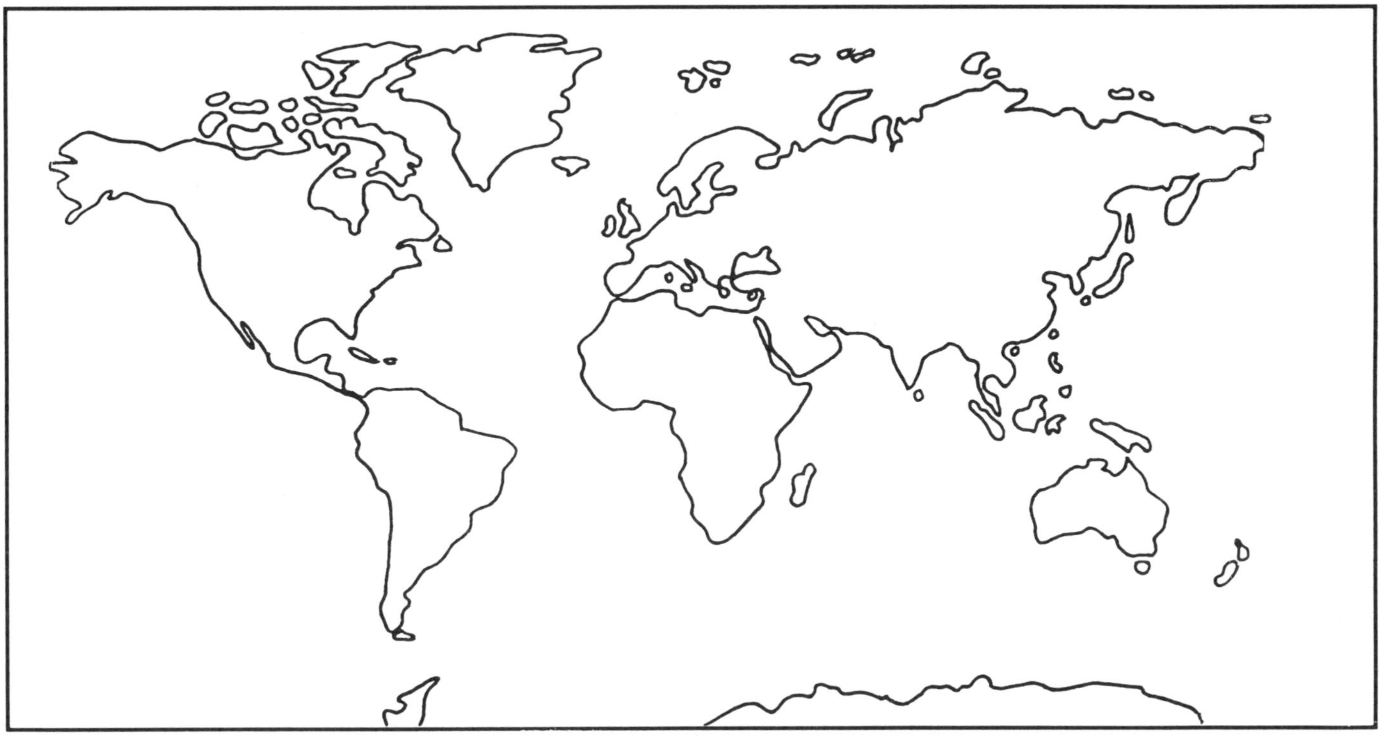

China City-dwellers are five times more likely to die of lung cancer from air pollution.

Hungary
40% above the acceptable limits of pollution in the air and water.

LONDON 1956
Smog covers city. Deaths from bronchitis increase. 4 000 died.

UNITED STATES OF AMERICA
150 million citizens daily breathe 'officially' unhealthy air.

RUSSIA
In 102 cities air pollution is often ten times above the limits for healthy air.

MEXICO CITY
School children are given a whole month off school because the air is so polluted.

- Find out about the London smogs of the 1950s. What was done to stop them from happening again?

Acid Rain - Ideas Page

Aim

- To help children to understand how acid rain forms, and what is being done to combat the problem.

Background

In 1872, an English chemist described the characteristics of acid rain. The gases which create acid rain are given off when fossil fuels, e.g. coal and oil, are burnt. The waste gases join with water vapour, sunlight and oxygen to make sulphuric and nitric acids. This mixture combines with water droplets, and reaches the earth's surface as rain or snow.

Activities

- Discuss the picture with the class or group. It may be useful to highlight technical words, e.g. gases, acid, chemical change, poisonous, acidified.
- Ask the children what they think these words mean, and make sure everyone can read the captions.
- Invite different children to describe the drawing 'The Acid Rain Story' before they begin the matching exercise.
- Identify and discuss the various stages of the process. Choose one of the pictures. Talk about it and ask volunteers to choose a suitable caption. Cut out the caption and paste it at the edge of the picture, attaching it to the corresponding image with a piece of string and a drawing pin.

Developments

- Do the children know what an acid is? If not, either make some cabbage indicator water or use universal indicator paper to illustrate acidity.
- To make indicator water use: half a red cabbage, a chopping surface, a blunt knife, warm water, a bowl to soak the chopped cabbage in, a sieve, a plastic beaker/jug and a separate jug to collect the cabbage water.
  - Chop the cabbage and soak it in warm (not boiling) water until the liquid turns purple.
  - Sieve the water, and collect it in a container.
  - Throw away the chopped cabbage caught in the sieve.

- Investigate everyday chemicals for acidity. Make a collection of: vinegar, lemonade, washing-up liquid, milk, lemon juice and water. Measure samples into small pots or a clean paint palette and label each one. Use one sample of cabbage water as a 'control'. Add a small amount of cabbage water (using a pipette or dropper) to each chemical. Compare the samples to the control to see if there has been any colour change.
- Place the same amount of the kitchen chemical, e.g. bleach, in a separate dish. Add a small amount of cabbage water. What happens? If the cabbage turns pink, it means that the solution is acidic. Did the children manage to work this out?
- Acid is measured on a pH scale 1-14. Healthy lakes and rivers are usually non-acidic. They should measure 5.6 - 8 on the pH scale. Rain is naturally very weakly acidic, about pH 5.6. Children could collect samples of rainwater and record the pH. Does it change at different times of the day or the week, or during different weather conditions?

The Acid Rain Story

- Describe what is shown in the different parts of the picture.
- Read the captions below, cut them out and place them next to the correct part of the picture.

Gases from factories and power stations pass into the air.	Sunlight causes chemical changes to take place in the air.
Exhaust fumes, gases like sulphur dioxide and nitrogen oxide, rise into the air.	Gases and acid in the air damage trees. They lose their leaves and die.
Gases in the air and acids in the rain damage buildings.	Sulphuric acid and nitric acid are in the rainwater - 'acid rain'.
Trees take up acid in the water they absorb from the soil.	Lakes and underground water stores are made acid.
Acid rain falls on soil, which becomes acidified.	People may be harmed by acid in the air and water.

The Greenhouse Effect - *Ideas Page*

Aim

- To introduce children to the concept of 'The Greenhouse Effect' and its effect upon our environment.

Background

The atmosphere prevents the earth from becoming too warm by keeping out most of the sun's heat. Usually, it allows heat to escape into space, cooling the earth. However, carbon dioxide gases prevent the heat from escaping - so the earth may gradually be warming up - 'The Greenhouse Effect'.
In 1896, a Swedish chemist called Svante Arrhenius named 'The Greenhouse Effect'. He correctly predicted that using fossil fuels would:
- increase the amount of CO_2 in the atmosphere
- lead to the warming of the world's climate.

CO_2 is produced by: exhaust fumes, aircraft, ships, motor transport, some industries, and homes. The decomposition and burning of felled trees is another source of CO_2.
Alternative sources of energy need to be found for transport and heating. Nuclear power, wind, wave or solar power may provide solutions to this problem. Planting more trees is also important because they use CO_2 in the process of photosynthesis.

Activities

- Introduce the concept of 'The Greenhouse Effect' by demonstrating the following experiment. Collect two small glass jars, a jug of water, a polythene bag and two thermometers. Half fill each jar. Cover one of these loosely with the polythene bag. Record the temperature of the water. Place both jars in the sun for an hour. Record the temperature of the water again. (The water in the jar with the polythene cover will be warmer.)

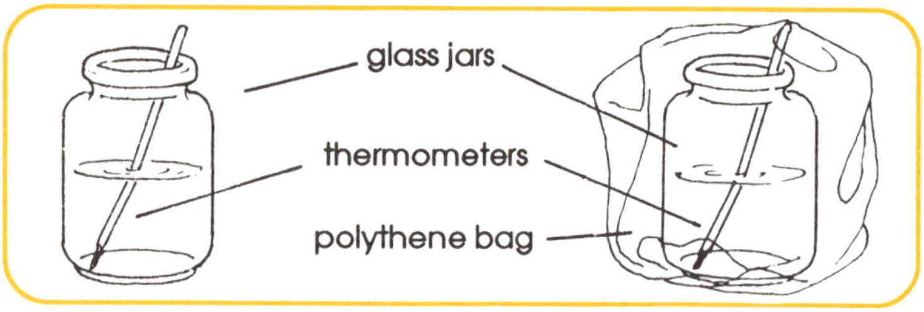

Before carrying out the experiment, ask children to guess what will happen. Did they predict a temperature rise? The polythene bag represents the gases released into the atmosphere when fossil fuels are burnt. These gases have built up, keeping the heat in, and as a result warming the earth. This global warming may in time cause the polar icecaps to melt. If this happens, the sea level will rise and many areas could be flooded.

- Work on the activity sheet as a group, using the information in the background box for a discussion of how carbon dioxide is created, and how this production could be reduced.

Developments

- Talk about the effects of melting icecaps. Look at an atlas or globe. What will more water in the seas mean? Which countries may be flooded? Help the children to locate low-lying coastal areas, such as the Nile Delta and Bangladesh.
- Provide children with some facts:
  - The 1980s were, on average, the hottest ten years ever recorded.
  - The world has become warmer by 0.3°C - 0.6°C in the last 100 years.
  - Scientists suggest that by AD2020 the world will be 1.3°C warmer than it is now.
  - By AD2070, it will be 3°C warmer.
- Children could draw a block graph to show this data.
- The graphs should show that in:
  - 100 years the temperature rose 0.5°C.
  - in another 30 years there will be a 1.3°C rise.

The Greenhouse Effect

The sun heats the earth. Carbon dioxide made from fuels we burn rises and is absorbed into the atmosphere. This prevents heat from escaping into space.

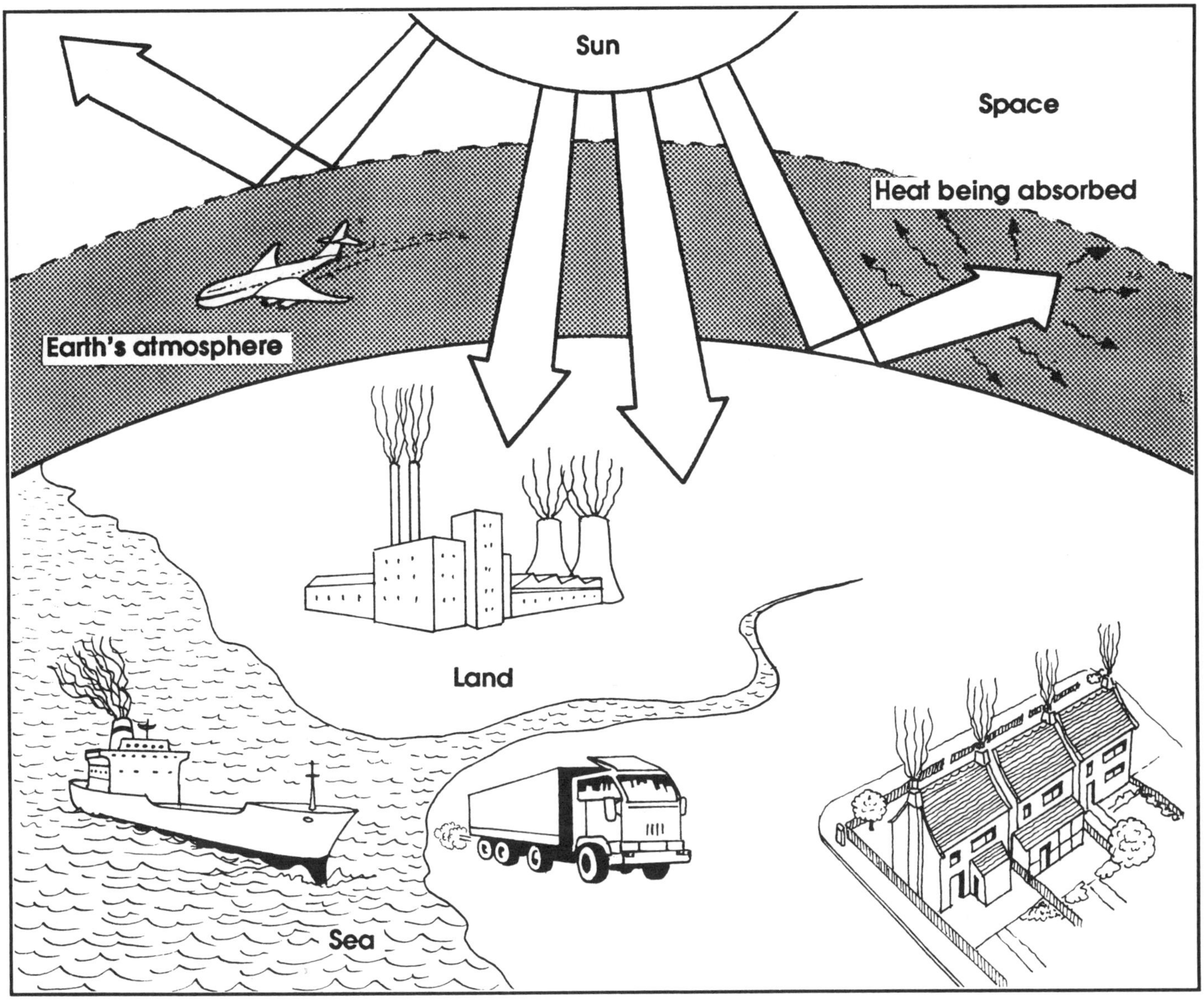

- Find out where carbon dioxide (CO_2) is made, and make a list.
- What could be done to stop so much carbon dioxide from being made?

Notes

Aim

- To bring to children's attention the fact that many everyday items and procedures are environmentally harmful.

Activities

- All the items shown on the activity sheet could affect the ozone layer because of their contents and packaging. Suggest that children look at empty aerosols to see if they claim to be 'ozone-friendly'.
- Identify the items in the drawings, and their uses. Collect empty containers to remind children of the way in which these products are packaged.

- Children could design a questionnaire to find out how many people use products which are harmful to the environment.
- Cut out relevant magazine or newspaper articles and paste or pin them on to a notice board, or make them into a class reference book entitled 'Harmful Wastes Book'.

Background

The earth is wrapped in a layer of protective gas called ozone, written in chemical symbols as O_3. This layer forms a life-saving protective shield 15-50 kilometres above the earth's surface, in the stratosphere. It filters out some of the deadly ultraviolet rays of the sun. However, this protective layer is very thin and has holes in it. The holes are thought to have been caused by harmful chemicals, especially CFCs (chlorofluorocarbons).
In 1982, a British scientific expedition found that much of the ozone above the Antarctic had disappeared. They thought their instruments were malfunctioning, but successive tests in 1983 and 1984 found that there was less and less ozone. When they published their results there was an uproar.
CFCs are chemicals which have been used in many everyday products, e.g. as the propellant for deodorants and hair sprays. Other harmful chemicals in our environment include fertilizers and pesticides. Both of these were designed to be helpful to the world, but over use has resulted in:
- pests becoming increasingly immune to pesticides, e.g. mosquitoes have become resistant to DDT
- poisons being absorbed by the soil and entering the water cycle, affecting other living things.

Developments

- Ask children to find the definitions of 'fertilizer', and 'pesticide'. Why were these developed? Are there any circumstances where they could be beneficial?
- Provide the children with these figures:
  - In 1950, 14 million metric tonnes of fertilizer were used worldwide.
  - In 1989, 143 million metric tonnes were used.

  (This is the equivalent of 5kg per person in 1950, and 25kg per person in 1989.) What has happened to the amount of fertilizer used? Ask children to suggest reasons for such a large increase, e.g. more sophisticated farming methods.
- Children could design a poster to warn people that fertilizer use has increased.
- What would happen if we stopped using fertilizers in the world? Ask the children to research 'biological control', e.g. ladybirds eat greenfly. Is this a realistic way to reduce the use of pesticides?

- There are internationally recognised symbols for toxic chemicals. Ask the children to find out what they are.

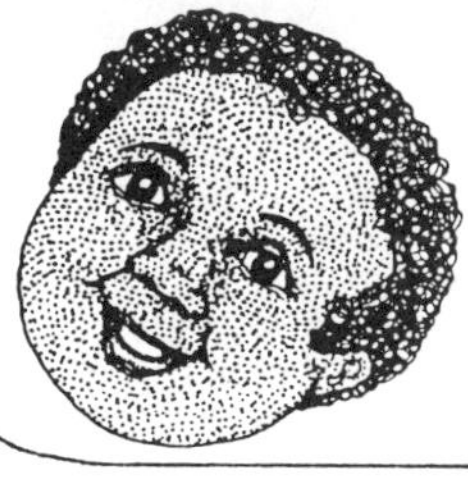

Harmful Wastes

Many products we use in everyday life release harmful wastes into the air. The products shown on this sheet all contain chemicals called CFCs.

- Do you use any of these products, or have you seen them on sale anywhere?
- Collect labels and empty containers of aerosol products.
- Design and carry out a survey to find out which of these products contain harmful CFCs. You may need to read the labels carefully.

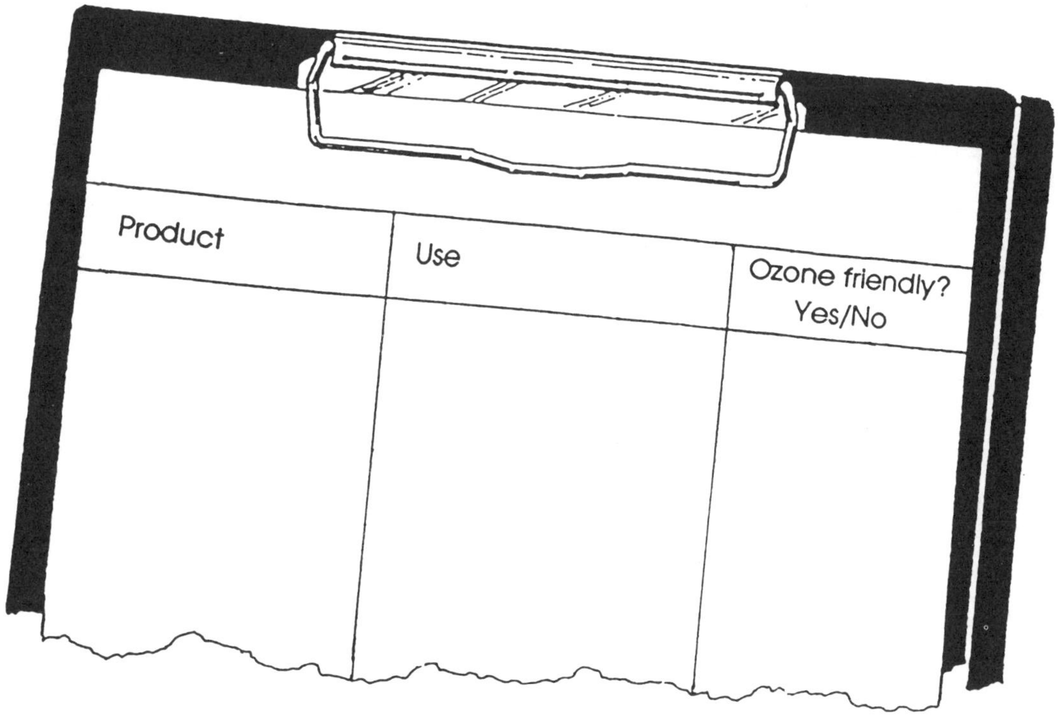

NOW

- Research the ozone layer. Why are people so concerned about the effects of CFCs?

Conserving Habitats - Ideas Page

Aim

- To help children find out about the causes of changes in the landscape, which in turn affect where living things can exist.

Background

Large areas of the earth's land surface are turning into desert. One third of all land is under threat. It is impossible to farm these areas unless water, fertilizers and able-bodied workers are available.
Many crucial habitats are being destroyed by human activity. Mangrove swamps and coral reefs are among the world's most important threatened habitats; rainforests are another.
Mangrove trees grow at the edge of the sea, and their roots provide places for fish to live. At the same time they filter out pollution and stop the shoreline from being eroded.
Coral reefs are one of the oldest natural living systems. Most reefs are between 5 000 and 10 000 years old. Only the surface of a reef is living, the rest is the 'skeletons' of former animals. These habitats are very rich in wildlife, and often support up to 3 000 different species. Coral reefs are also useful sources of medicine, prevent coastal erosion and are tourist attractions.

Activities

- Desert is created when trees are cut down on a large scale. The wind rushes across the surface of the bare land, drying out and blowing away the topsoil. Deforestation also means that water runs off the land, washing away topsoil. If this land is grazed too heavily new trees do not develop and desertification may follow.
- Show the children some pictures of fertile land, deserts and seashores which have been developed. Who is gaining from these activities? Point out the short term effects of building tourist homes on a tropical beach, e.g. the beach will become polluted and wildlife will suffer.

Developments

- Simulate the effects of soil erosion by pouring water (heavy rain) down a sloped piece of card with damp sand on it (a hillside). Make the experiment more realistic by giving the hillside an uneven surface, then prop up the piece of card to form a slope. Pour water slowly on to the middle of the sand at the top of the slope. When the jug is empty, the children could tilt the board to one side and see what happens.

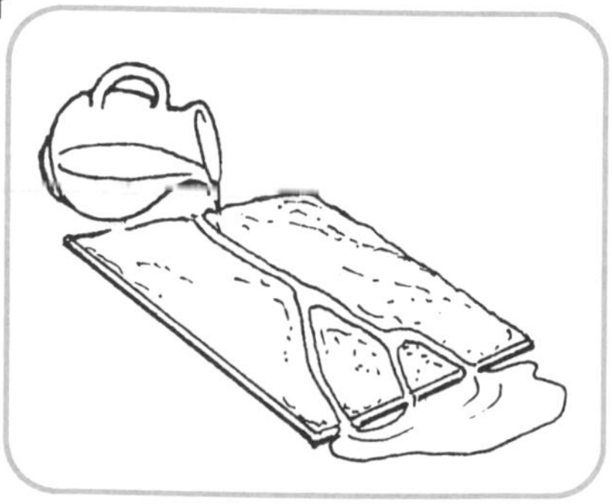

- What are the children's observations? The water finds the easiest path down and washes away any loose sand. If the board is tilted, the water finds a new path.
- Ask the children how they could investigate the effect of cutting down trees. They might use the same equipment, with sticks to represent trees. One side of the board could have 'trees' whilst the other is bare. How could they make this a fair test?
- Ask children to collect photographs of places which are considered to be unspoilt. Talk about their pictures. Now add a cut-out of some new item, e.g. a factory or a hotel. What effect would this have? Who would benefit?

Conserving Habitats

The world is changing all the time. Sometimes human beings cause changes which damage the environment.

From this ——▷ to this.

WHY?

Look at the pictures above. Here are four reasons which may have caused the environment to change.

- [ ] Too much farming on poor soil
- [ ] Cutting down trees for fuel, leaving the soil bare
- [ ] Bad irrigation (watering) methods
- [ ] Over grazing of grasslands.

- Talk about the reasons in a group, and number them in order of importance. 1 should be the most important.

From this ——▷ to this.

NOW • Try to explain what has happened to the beach environment.

Disasters - Ideas Page

Aim

- To explain that some disasters are created by human beings.
  Disasters affect all living things, but nature recovers from natural disasters much more easily than those caused by human activities.

Background

Volcanoes are found on the earth's crust, particularly where there are faults, or lines of weakness. The molten material, magma, from inside the earth, is able to push up through the surface, and the volcano erupts.
Other natural disasters include earthquakes (when the 'plates' which form the earth's crust move), floods, hurricanes, tornadoes and fires.
Disasters created by humans affect the habitats of other living things, e.g. oil tankers breaking up at sea cause the pollution of wide stretches of coastline.

Activities

- Children will need to be provided with appropriate reference material for the first part of activity. Then help them to name the parts of the volcano.
- Recreate a volcanic eruption, using a washing-up liquid bottle. This may give the children a sense of its force. Stand the bottle in a bowl. Add wo teaspoons of bicarbonate of soda to a one quarter full bottle of warm soapy (detergent) water. Add 15ml of vinegar. Stand back! Emphasise that children should not repeat this experiment at home without the supervision of an adult.

- Once the children have discussed the two types of disasters, make separate lists of the effects.

Developments

- Volcanic eruptions have occurred throughout human history. Ask the children to research some famous ones, particularly Vesuvius.

  One group could produce a TV bulletin, whilst another group writes a newspaper report about the eruption and its effect on the people of Pompeii.
- Find the location of volcanoes and mark them on a world map. Do they form a pattern? Is it possible to draw lines to show where the weaknesses in the earth's crust lie?
- Children could find out about the Richter Scale, and what it is used to measure (the magnitude of an earthquake).
  Tremors of 2.0 or less are called micro-earthquakes. They are not commonly felt by people. Tremors of 4.5 or more are strong enough to be recorded all over the world.
- Oil has a devastating effect on sea life. Demonstrate this to the class:
  - Collect some bird feathers.
  - Ask the children to examine them using a hand lens.

  - Drop water on to a feather. What do the children notice? Why must the feathers be waterproof?
  - Immerse the feather in cooking oil. What happens? What happens if water is dropped on to the feather? The feather lets water through. Therefore, a bird with oil-clogged feathers would soon becomes wet and as a result would loose body heat.
- Birds cannot fly with oil-clogged feathers. Ask children how this would affect these animals. Can children think of ways in which the oil could be removed? (Conservationists use detergent.)

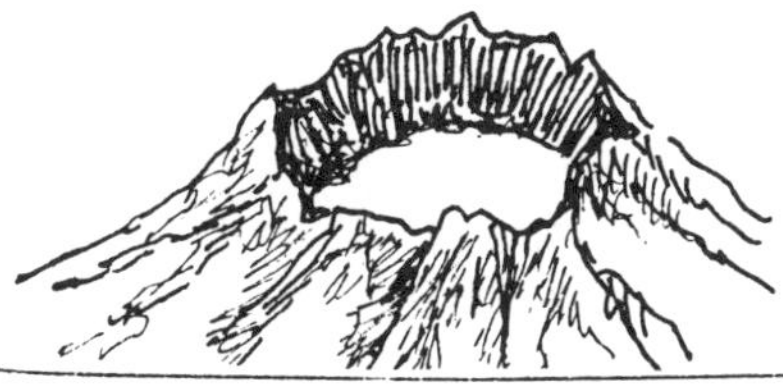

Disasters

Natural disasters are caused by the planet and its surroundings. However, some disasters are caused by human beings.

- Talk about the effects of a volcanic eruption on the environment.
- Label the diagram of the volcano using the words in the box below.

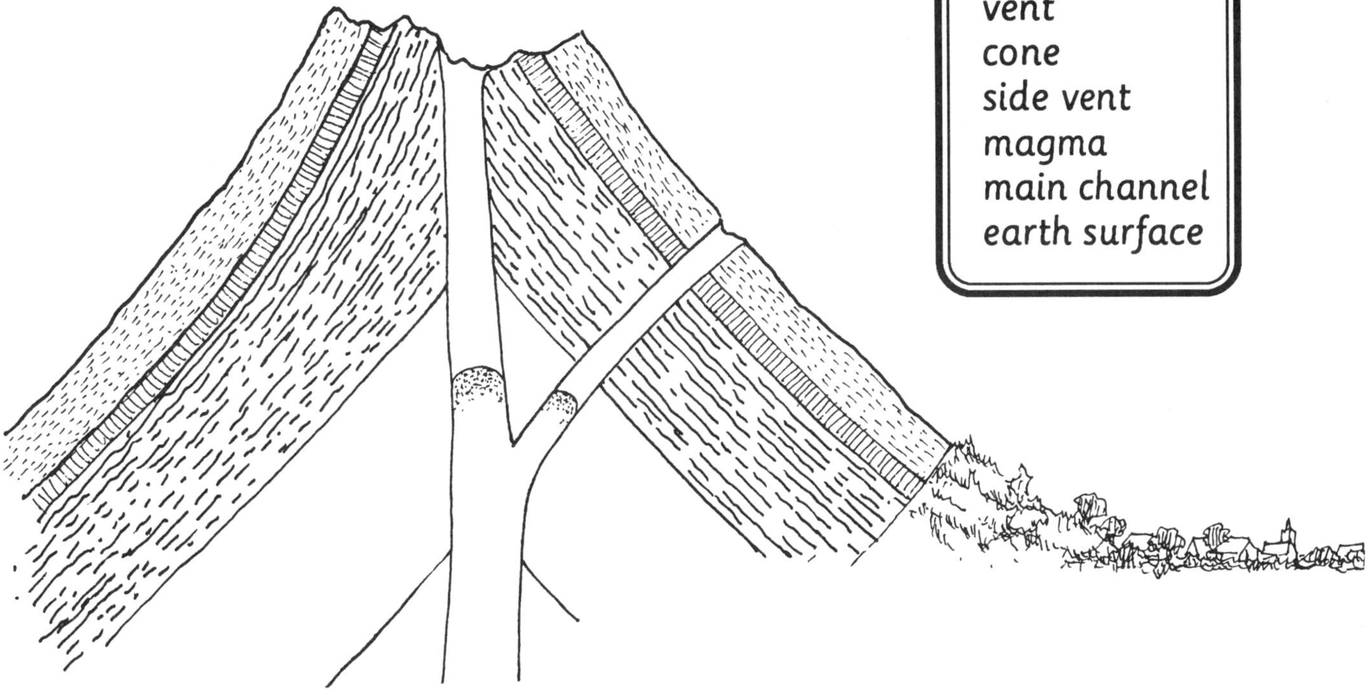

vent
cone
side vent
magma
main channel
earth surface

NOW

- How might the oil escaping from this tanker affect:
  - -humans
  - -plants
  - -mammals
  - -fish
  - -birds
  - -the air?

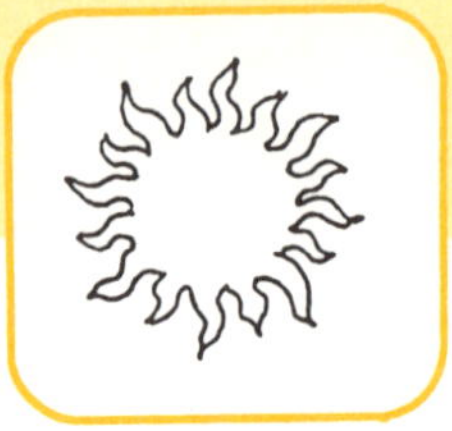

Aim

- To explain the characteristics of food chains, and the fact that ultimately all energy comes from the sun.

Background

All energy in livings things comes from the sun. Sunlight causes certain chemicals to combine to make carbohydrates, sugars and starches. These chemicals store the sun's energy. This chemical bonding only occurs in green plants, and is called photosynthesis. Animals obtain this energy by eating green plants or other animals which have eaten stored energy.
The order in which living things are eaten is called a food chain, or a food web. Plant eaters, e.g. a rabbit, are known as primary consumers. Meat eaters are secondary consumers (carnivores). Animals which eat carnivorous animals are called tertiary consumers.

Activities

Answers:
The rabbit, snail, earthworm and caterpillar are primary consumers. The thrush, human and dung beetle are secondary consumers. The fox and human may be tertiary consumers.

- Before giving children the activity sheet, explain the terms primary, secondary and tertiary consumer.

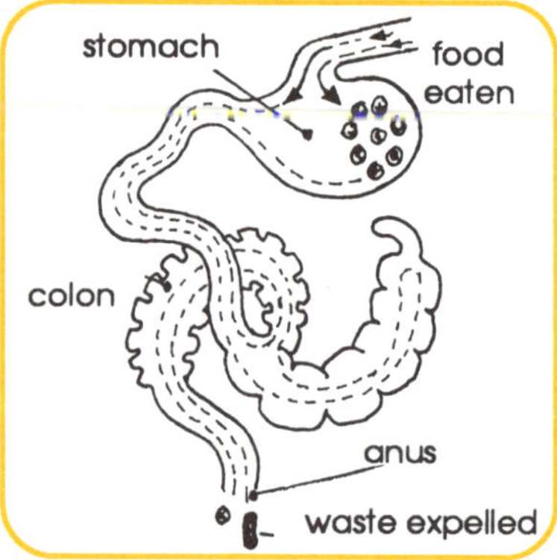

- Explain the process of digestion. Animals eat food, this passes through the gut, in which the energy (in the form of chemicals) is removed. Waste products are then expelled from the anus. Also explain that all living things die and the chemicals which they are made of are broken down and re-used.

Developments

- Talk about other food chains, e.g. in Antarctica:

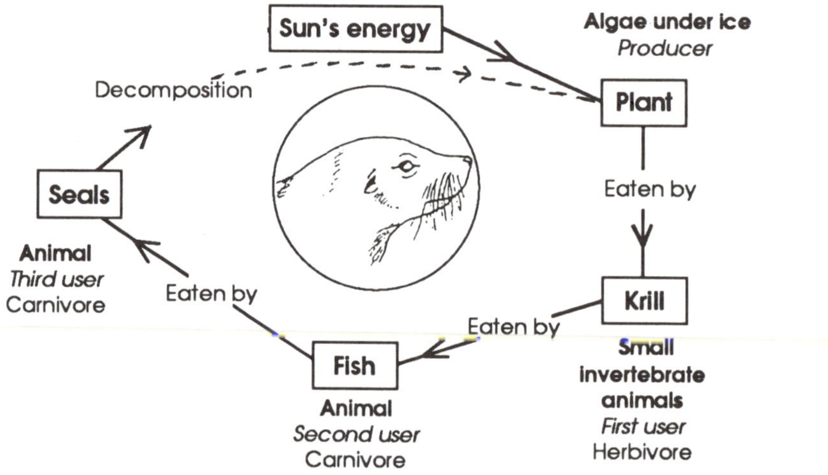

- Ask children to work out the food chain for one of their meals, e.g. breakfast. They could draw pictures of stages in the sequence on to pieces of card, and tie them on to a coat hanger. These could be suspended from the classroom ceiling.

- Provide the children with a copy of this statement made by Chief Seattle (1788-1866): 'Man did not weave the web of life. He's merely a strand of it. Whatever he does to the web of life he does to himself.' What message do they think he was trying to communicate?
- Suppose some kind of pollution, e.g. pesticide was introduced into the food chain. What happens? Could the process be stopped once it had begun?

Food Chains

Energy comes from the sun and is stored in plants.
It may pass along a chain of animals before reaching us.
If an animal eats a plant it is called a primary consumer.
If this animal eats another animal it is called a secondary consumer.
- *What is an animal called which eats a secondary consumer?*

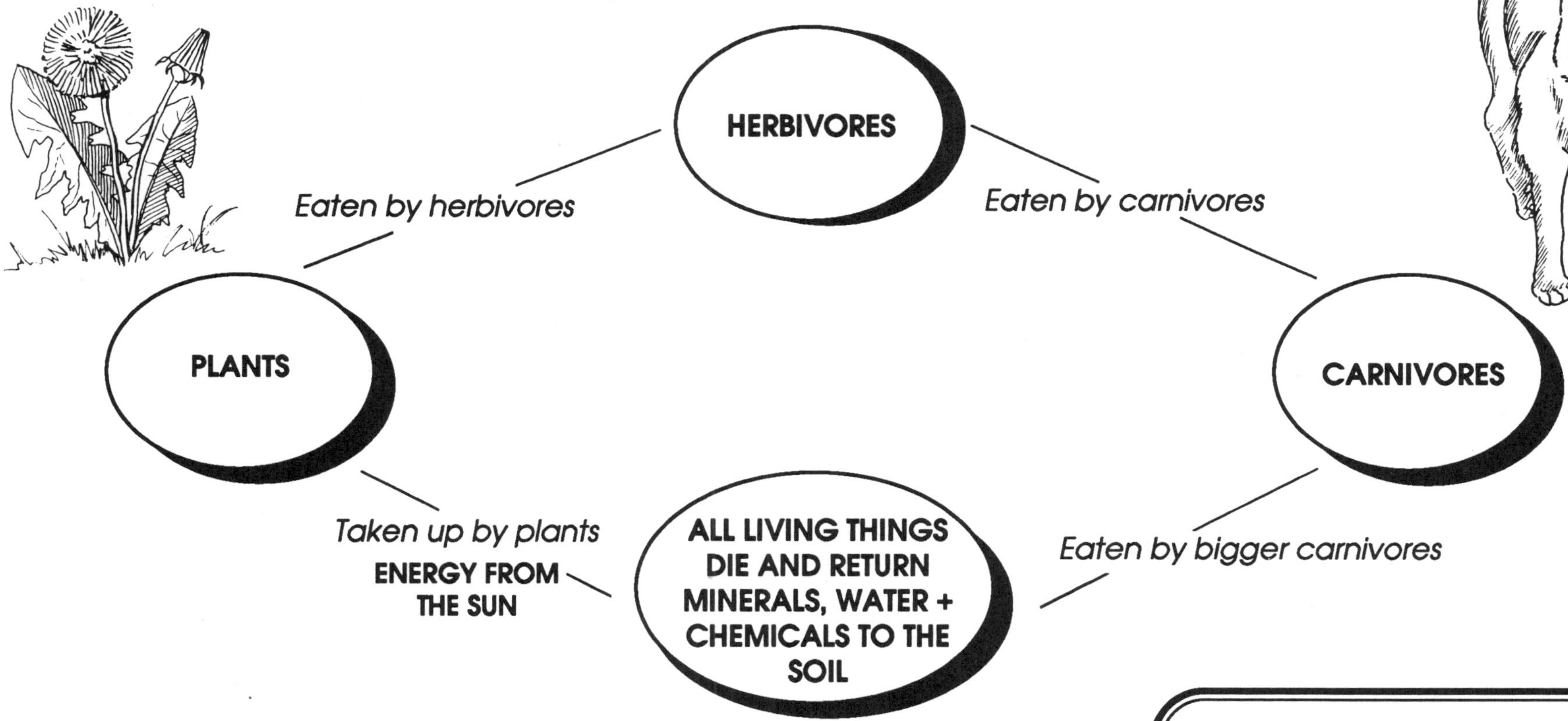

NOW

- Draw the animals listed in the box in the correct places on the energy circle.
- Write next to them whether they are primary, secondary or tertiary consumers.

ANIMALS:
Fox, thrush, snail, rabbit, earthworm, caterpillar, human, dung beetle.

Recycling - Ideas Page

Aims

- To identify recyclable items of waste.
- To find out about recycling in the local community.

Background

Humans produce vast amounts of waste, much of this is just thrown away. In nature there is no waste. Things are reused, although they may be broken into their individual components first. In an industrialised country a typical family of four people throws away 2 tonnes of waste per year. Much of this is buried in landfill sites, even though many items could have been recycled. Recycling does use energy. Sometimes it is more efficient **not** to recycle all waste.

Activities

Answers:
Newspapers. Bundle and give them to recyclers. Use them for wrapping.
Plastic bottles. Use for other jobs or take them to a plastic recycler.
Clear glass. Reuse or take to a glass collection unit.
Coloured glass. Use for other tasks or collect and take to a coloured glass collection unit.
Clothing. Use for fillings or rugmaking. Donate to charity. Collect and take to a clothing recycling point.
Aluminium (drinks cans). Collect and clean them. Take to a recycling point.
Tin cans. Collect and clean them. Take to a recycling point.
Vegetable matter. Make a compost heap.

- Before starting the activity, ask children to make a list of the waste they think they produce every day.
- Provide children with maps of the local neighbourhood, and ask them to locate and mark recycling points.
- The children will have many ideas for ways of separating the waste. One common idea is to design a conveyor belt. A magnet collects non-aluminium cans, and aluminium cans and bottles fall down a hole. Newspapers are collected in a large box at the end of the conveyor belt.

Developments

- Examine books, notepaper and packaging to see how many are made from recycled material? Is there a special symbol for this? Ask children to design other suitable logos.
- Worm waste users! Worms are valuable to the environment, as they convert disposable matter into new substances. Make a wormery so that children are able to observe the behaviour of these creatures:
  - Collect a variety of soils, e.g. chalk, clay, humus and garden soil (use plastic gloves when handling soil).
  - Place the soil in layers in a tank.
  - Collect some plant waste, e.g. potato peelings, and weigh it. Then add this to the wormery along with approximately 0.5kg of worms.

  The wormery must be kept at a temperature around 28ºC. Also, remember to keep the soil moist, because worms only obtain sugar (and remove waste gas and carbon dioxide) through their skin when it is damp.

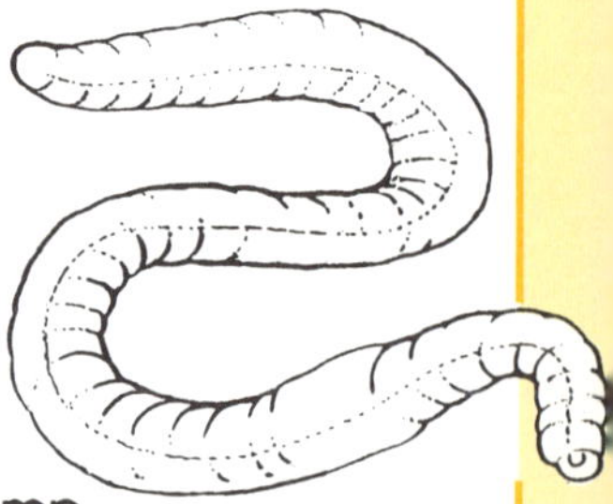

- 0.5kg of earthworms will recycle about 4.25kg of waste per day. Children could work out the feeding capacity of the wormery using these figures and the weight of plant waste added to the wormery.
- Children could measure the temperature in the middle of the worm bin at regular intervals. Why does it rise?

Time	Temperature (ºC)
10.00am	26
12.00am	26.2
1.00pm	26.4

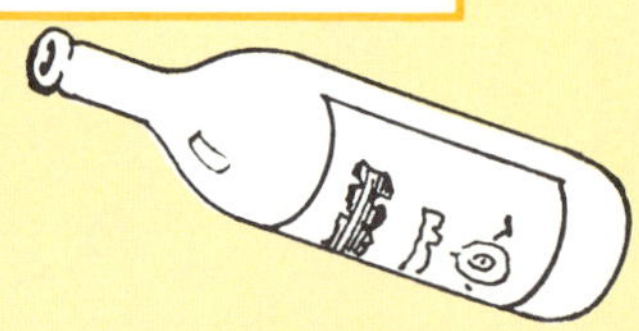

Recycling

- Work in pairs. Complete the chart.

Item	How would you prepare this/these for recycling?	Your nearest recycling centre
Newspapers		
Plastic bottles		
Clear glass		
Coloured glass		
Clothing		
Aluminium		
Tin cans		
Vegetable matter.		

NOW

- Design a way of separating three items of waste, e.g. aluminium drinks cans, tin cans and newspaper, during the recycling process.

Waste - Ideas Page

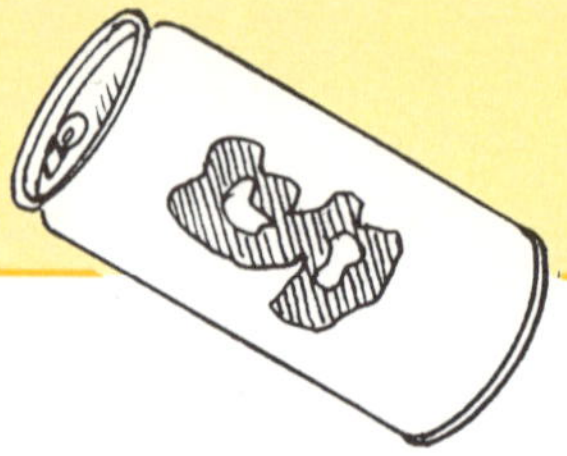

Aim

- To make children aware that not all waste decomposes naturally, and something that seems insignificant, such as litter, is an environmental issue.

Background

All living things produce waste. This, together with the remains of the organism is broken down by the action of scavengers, e.g. vultures, burying beetles and 'the decomposers' - bacteria and fungi.
Non-living materials take a lot longer to break down, or do not decompose at all. These manufactured products may be recycled and used again, but this takes organisation, uses energy, and costs money. However, if these items continue to be buried, logically, one day the earth will be full.

Activities

Answers:

- The items shown on the activity sheet would decompose over the following periods of time:

Sandwich	1 month
Paper napkins	1 year
Orange peel	2 years
Newspaper	5 years
Plastic bag	20 years
Tin can	50 years
Aluminum drinks can	500 years
Glass bottle	1 000 years.

- Before starting this activity, demonstrate how things decompose, e.g. bring some bread or a piece of fruit into the class for children to watch over a period of time. They could make diaries to show day-by-day changes. Talk about their observations.
- Discuss the work of archaeologists, and how something may be preserved in soil for long periods of time. Ask children to list famous examples from history, such as the Tollund Man.

Developments

- Carry out a survey of waste found in the school environment.
  - Locate waste bins and mark them on a map of the school.
  - Empty the contents of a wastebin on to paper or sheeting.
  - Ask children to examine the waste, and to identify items (using sticks). They should all be wearing plastic gloves.
  - Children could group together similar items, e.g. plant waste, paper, fabric, and record what they have found.
  - Place each set of materials in a polythene bag and weigh them. What did each group of waste weigh?
  - Ask children to suggest ways of presenting and analysing the results.

- Children could design a strategy for the more effective recycling of waste material in the school environment. This may include collection points for different types of waste, and posters displayed around the school to show other children where to put their litter. This could be in the form of a list of do's and don'ts.
- Find out about landfill sites. Locate any in the local area. Are they near to housing developments? Do they provide any safeguards to protect the local environment? Children could investigate whether there are any initiatives for recycling on-site.

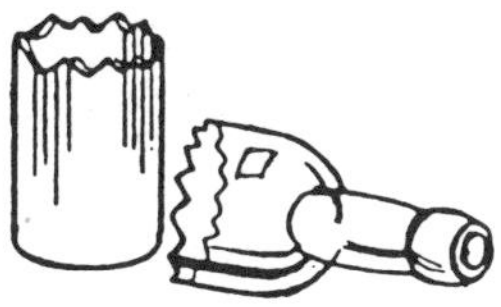

Waste

Some waste is buried. It takes a long time to rot away.
Some will never disappear.

- Make a 'Waste Away' time line:
  - Cut out and attach the date labels to a piece of string, in date order. These show how long it takes for different items to rot away.
  - Cut out the items of waste and paste each one next to what you think is the correct date label.

1 month	1 year	2 years	5 years
20 years	50 years	500 years	1 000 years

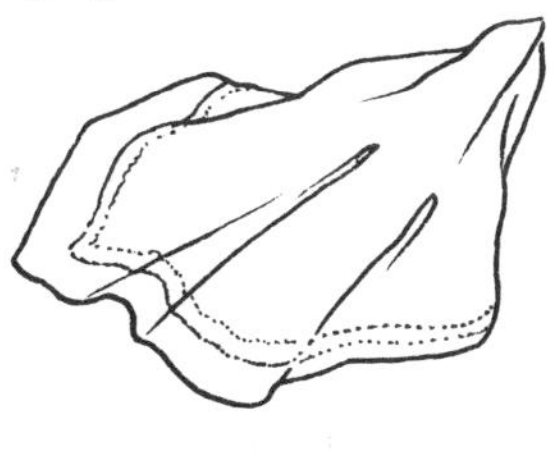
Paper napkin

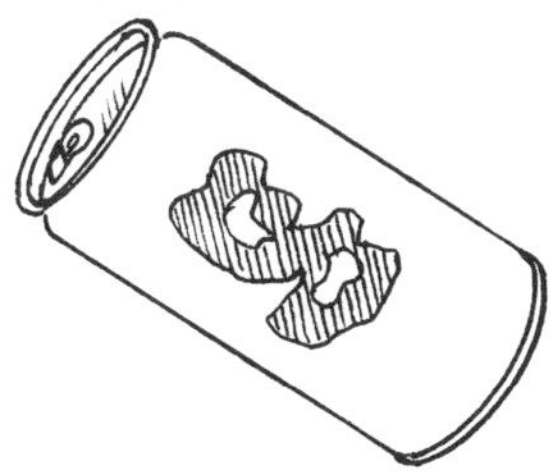
Aluminium can

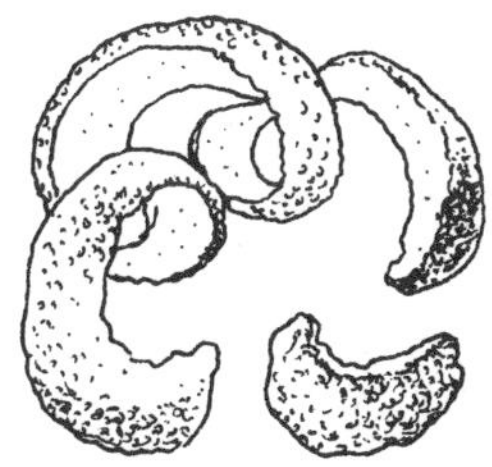
Orange peel

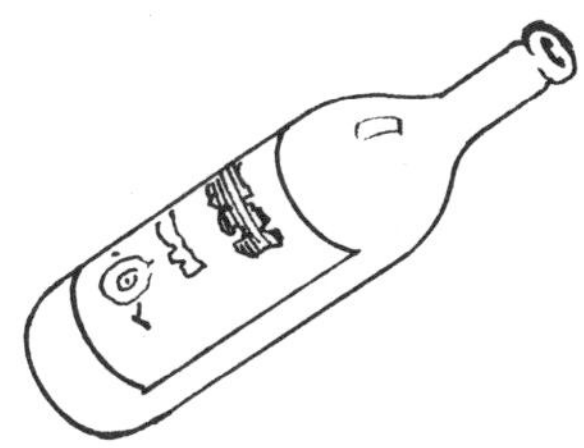
Glass bottle

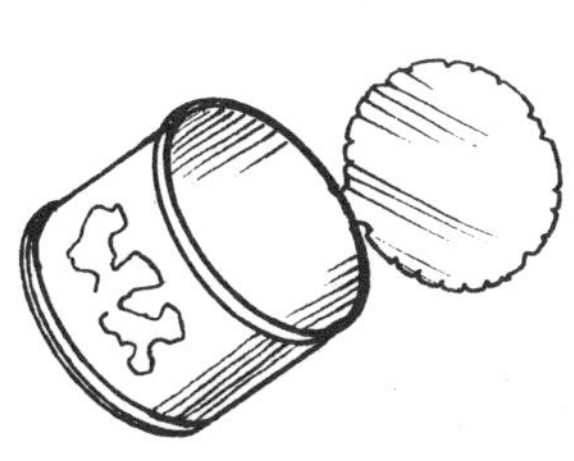
Tin can

Plastic bag

Newspaper

Sandwich

- Compare your 'Waste Away' time line with another group's. Talk about the differences.

Energy - Ideas Page

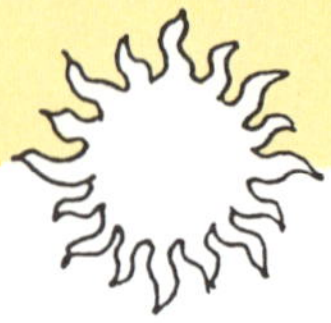

Aim

- To introduce children to renewable sources of energy.

Activities

Answers:
It is important to locate the windmill on a suitable site. It must be away from obstruction. Site **A** is unsuitable because the lowest part of the 'mill', or blades, should be 7 metres above any obstruction within a 100 metre radius. It is better to site a windmill at the top of a gentle slope because steep hills generate counter air currents. Therefore, **B** is an unsuitable site. Site **C** is the best place for a continuous air flow.

- Before starting this activity, talk about windmills:
  - What makes them move?
  - What are they used for?

- Ask the children what they think the advantages and disadvantages of alternative energy schemes might be e.g.
  - the cost of installing them
  - damage to wildlife habitats
  - alterations to the appearance of the landscape.

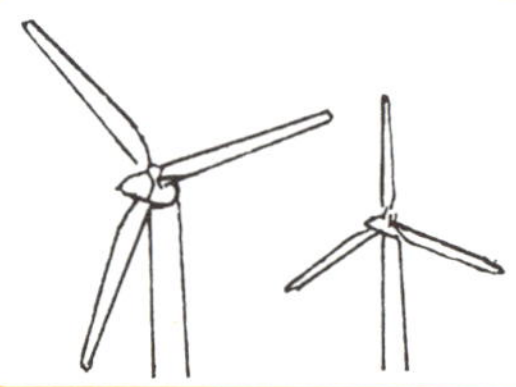

Background

The most common type of renewable energy is hydro power. This uses the power of water as it flows from high land to the sea. Tides move water to and from land twice a day. This large water movement can also be converted into electrical energy by turbines.
Windpower is an important source of energy. Potential energy is produced by the movement of the blades. Ninety-five percent of countries obtain some of their energy from the wind.
Solar panels on roofs collect the sun's rays and turn it into solar energy for heating water. The sun may be used to power many other things, e.g. calculators.
Geothermal power uses the heat from inside the earth. At the moment this source of energy can only be tapped where hot water reservoirs exist.

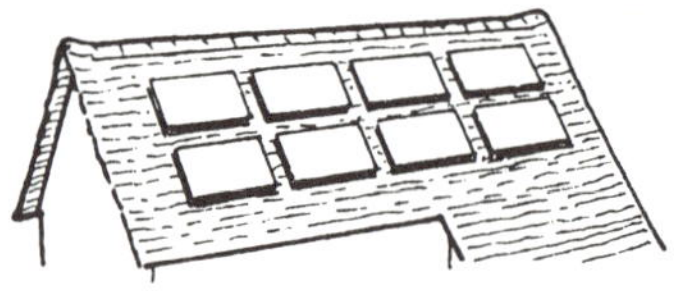

Developments

- Provide the children with the information in **A**, and locate the areas mentioned on a world map. Talk about the different kinds of power, how they are created and what they are used for in that particular area.

A

Cyprus	Solar powered homes heated by hot water.
Sweden Germany Denmark USA	Giant windmills use wind energy to generate electricity.
Norway	The first wave operated power plant (UK is planning one).
USA Netherlands	Have windmill farms to generate electricity.
California Denmark	Makes 90% of the world's wind energy. Produces 6% of the world's wind energy.
Hawaii	33%of its energy is produced from plant remains.

- Explain to children the fact that lead-free fuels are healthier for us and the environment. Where is lead-free fuel found? Does the local petrol station sell it? What campaigns are there to promote the use of this type of fuel?
- How could people save energy? Suggest turning heating down, dressing more warmly, closing windows, stopping draughts, turning off lights when they are not needed. The children could carry out a survey to see how many people actually try to save fuel.

Energy

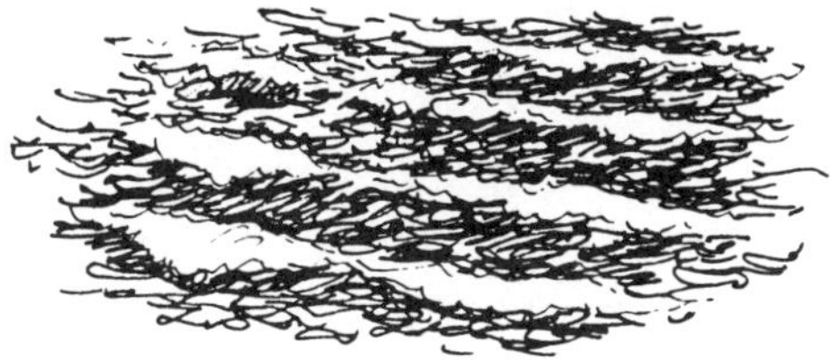

Some sources of energy can be used to create power again and again. These are called renewable resources.

- Carry out some research and fill in this chart.

Source of energy	How electricity is created from it	Advantages	Disadvantages
SUN WATER WIND TIDES WASTE			

These three pictures show places where a windmill could be sited.

- Talk about which is the best setting and why.

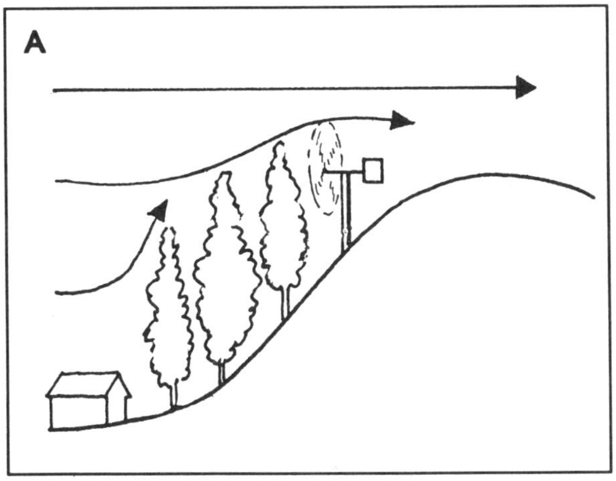

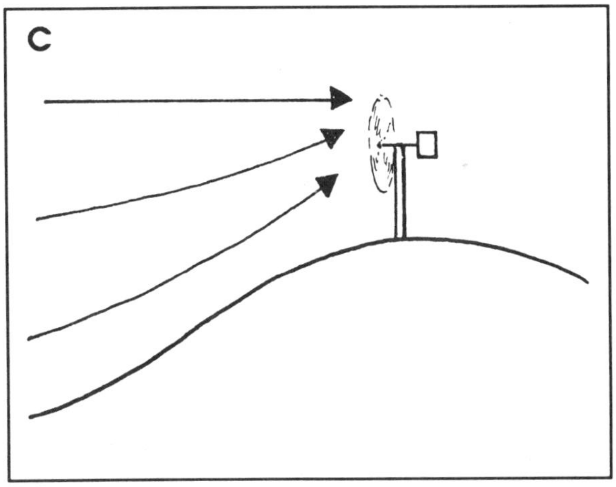

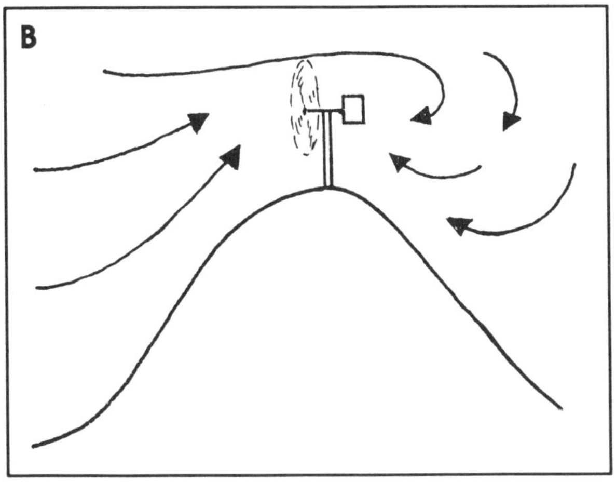

- Talk about why there are problems in using windpower as a major source of energy. Is it difficult to find sites for windmills?

Aim

- To explain to children that they are part of a larger environment. Meeting everyday needs has a direct effect on their environment.
- To show the children that environmental issues are all around them and they can have an effect on them.

Activities

- Before starting the activity, children could draw up two lists:
  - things essential to all living creatures
  - things which I need for my ideal world.
- Many of the items on their second list, e.g. TV, are not necessary to life. They do, however, affect the quality of life. Once you have discussed the basic biological needs to keep the body working, suggest the children work in a group to decide what other things are essential to their life, e.g. electricity, clothes.
- Ask children where the essential items come from. Prepare a sheet containing sentences such as:
  - I obtain food from...
  - I obtain oxygen from...
- The activity sheet gives the children an opportunity to identify environmental issues in their immediate environment, e.g. heat conservation, recycling, and to discuss how they can help to improve the situation.

Background

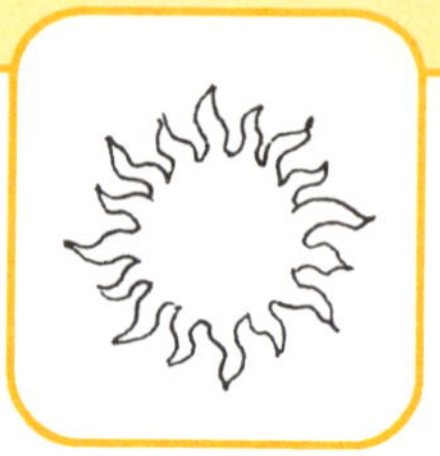

All living things share a number of needs:
- food
- water
- shelter/protection
- an air or oxygen supply (with very few exceptions).

They also need the sun, even if this energy is supplied indirectly through eating another living thing. If life is to continue, each living thing (unless it reproduces asexually) needs a partner for sexual exchange.
Part of this section focuses on the features of environments made by and for humans.

Developments

- Children could draw up their own contract: 'Ten things I will do over the next fourteen days to improve the environment in ... my bedroom, the classroom, the park.'
- Other plants and animals have basic needs. Examine a potted plant. Talk about what the plant needs to survive. Children could draw and label the different parts of the plant.

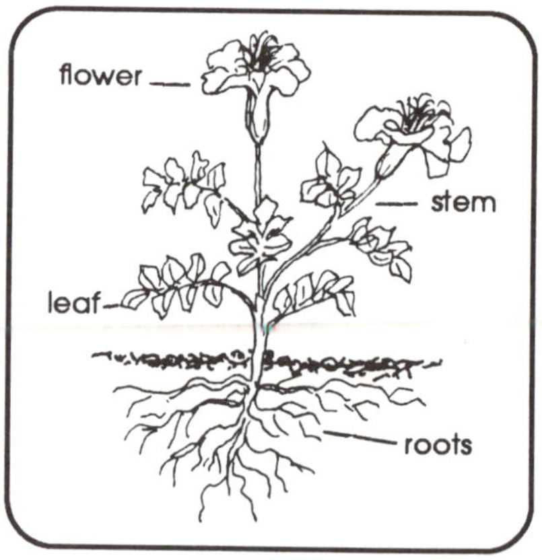

- Other animals have needs. Children could choose an animal, e.g. a goldfish, pony or cat, and then study the animal for several days in its environment. They could write a report of this animal's environment and how its needs are met. What role do humans play in the animal's survival?
- Suggest children find out about the history of their local area How has the area changed? What was built on the site of the school: 10, 20, 50 and 100 years ago?

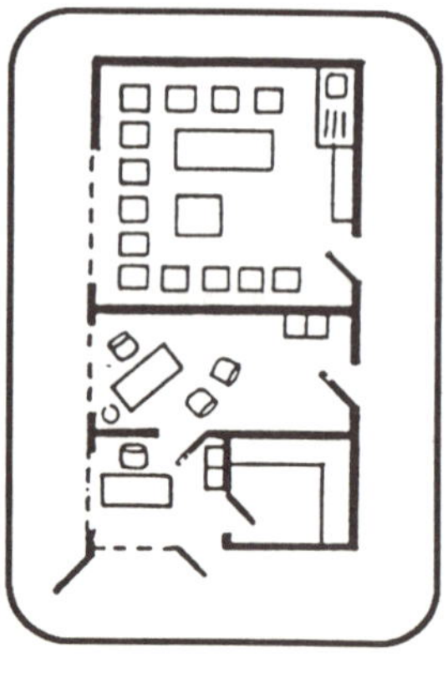

- Prepare an outline plan of the school and its grounds, so that the group could go on an 'Environment Safari' to find out where other things live. Discuss the children's observations. What could be done to attract more living things, e.g. make a special plant and butterfly garden?

My Environment

Look at the pictures below. They show two very different environments.

- For each of the environments talk about:
  - -any environmental issues you can see
  - -what you could do to help.

Aim

- To encourage children to take responsibility for the environment.

Background

Carl Sagan suggested there is no intelligent life on earth because of the way in which humans have destroyed their own environment.

The environment is in a balance and if human beings destroy too much, the balance is upset.

A native American of the Abernaki tribe said that there were four laws of nature:

1. There is no waste in nature.
2. Everything is connected.
3. There is no such place as 'away'.
4. The earth has limits - there is only so much we can use from the earth, and only so much waste we can put back.

Activities

- The pictures introduce ideas for saving water, heat, power and recycling at home. Talk about how these could be put into practice.
- Writing the postcard is a useful activity, because the children must be concise. These could be displayed under the title 'Saving My Environment'.

A Typical Wastebin

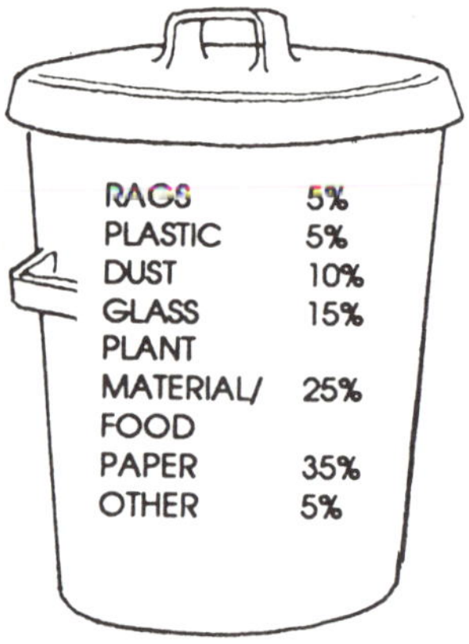

- Copy the diagram of 'A Typical Wastebin' for the children. Ask them what sort of things are thrown away the most and the least. What is thrown away most in the classroom? How could the children find out? If the majority of classroom litter is paper, ask the class to offer suggestions as to why. How could the amount of paper being disposed of be reduced?

Developments

- Suggest the children make a temperature diary for home or the classroom environment. They need to record the outside temperature too, and note what clothes they are wearing in class and outside in the playground.

Time	Temperature		Clothes worn	
	In class	Outside	In class	Outside

- What do the records tell the children? Is there any association between the temperature inside and outside and the type of clothes we wear? How could the children help by using less fuel to heat their environments?
- Children could check the labels on clothing, toys and foods at home. When they have collected these, provide them with a world map and an atlas. Ask them to find the country of origin of each product, and draw a line from there to their country. A rough estimate of distance can be obtained from the length of the line. Children could draw a distance chart based on this information.

- What type of environment do these products come from? Ask children to choose two of the countries of origin and research the local environments.
- Choose one item and invent its life history. Where did the material originate from? What travels did it go on? Who made it? Where was it bought? This activity could form the basis for a class display.

Saving My Environment

We can all help to save our environment by doing simple things.
Some of these are shown in the pictures below.

- List some reasons why these are useful steps to take.

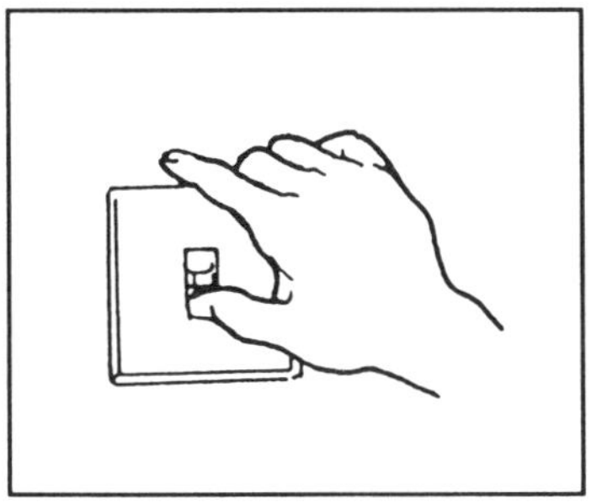

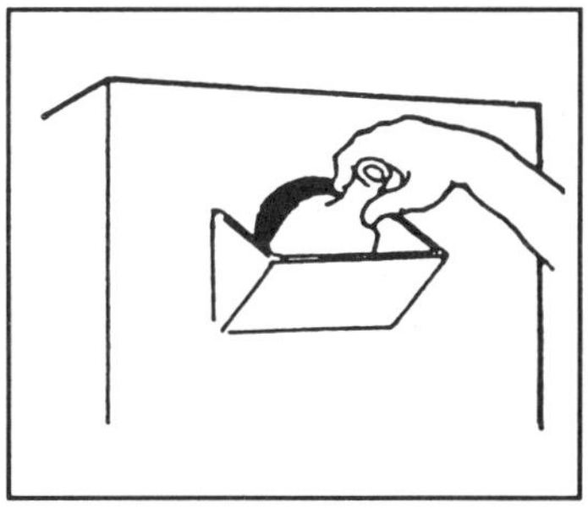

- Write a postcard to a world leader.
  How are you trying to save the environment?
  What could he or she do to help?

Eight ways to help ...

There are hundreds of ideas in this book to enable you to develop and extend the photocopiable pages. Here are just eight ways to help you make the most of the Ideas Bank series.

1

Photocopy a page, paste on to card and laminate/cover with sticky-backed plastic to use with groups. The children can now write on the pages using water-based pens which can be washed off.

2

Photocopy on to both sides of the paper, and put another useful activity on the back. Develop a simple filing system so that your colleagues can find relevant sheets and do not duplicate them again.

3

Save the sheets – if the children do not have to cut them up as a part of the activity – and re-use them. Label the sets, and keep them safely in files.

4

Make the most of group work. Children working in small groups need one sheet to discuss between them.

5

Put the sheets inside clear plastic wallets. This means the sheets are easily stored in a binder and will last longer. Again, the children's writing can be wiped away.

6

Use the activity page as an ideas page for yourself. Discuss issues with the class and ask the children to produce artwork and writing.

7

Make an overhead transparency of the page. You and your colleagues can now use the idea time and time again.

8

Ask yourself, "Does every child in this class/group need to deal with/work through this activity page?" If not, don't photocopy it!

